TRAVELS
WITH MY
SPATULA

RECIPES & STORIES FROM AROUND THE WORLD

Tori Haschka

Photography by Isobel Wield *Illustration by Andrea Turvey*

RYLAND PETERS & SMALL
LONDON • NEW YORK

dedication TO THE HUNGRY ONE

Senior Designer Megan Smith
Commissioning Editor
Céline Hughes
Production Controller
Gary Hayes
Art Director Leslie Harrington
Editorial Director Julia Charles

Prop Stylist Tony Hutchinson
Food Stylist Lizzie Harris
Indexer Hilary Bird

First published in 2013
This revised edition published in 2020
by Ryland Peters & Small
20–21 Jockey's Fields,
London WC1R 4BW
and
341 E 116th St
New York NY 10029

www.rylandpeters.com

10 9 8 7 6 5 4 3 2 1

Text © Tori Haschka 2013, 2020
Design and photographs ©
Ryland Peters & Small 2013, 2020

ISBN: 978-1-78879-209-7

Printed and bound in China

A CIP record for this book is
available from the British Library.

US Library of Congress Cataloging-
in-Publication Data has been
applied for.

Notes
• All spoon measurements are level,
unless otherwise specified.
• Recipes containing raw or
partially cooked egg, or raw fish
or shellfish, should not be served
to the very young, very old, anyone
with a compromised immune
system or pregnant women.
• All herbs are fresh, butter
unsalted and eggs UK medium or
US large unless otherwise stated.
• When a recipe calls for the grated
zest of citrus fruit, buy unwaxed
fruit and wash well before use.
If you can only find treated fruit,
scrub well in warm soapy water
and rinse before using.

CONTENTS

INTRODUCTION

'There is no love sincerer than the love of food.' GEORGE BERNARD SHAW (1856–1950)

Except perhaps a love of travel. Thank goodness the two go hand in hand.

My hunger for food and travel began when I found a co-pilot. We met in Sydney's inner west, in a dank pub with a Thai restaurant on the roof, its tables sticky from spilled drinks. Not long after, we went on a small adventure. After three days on the sands of Phuket spooning coconut tapioca and flat noodles with fiendishly hot chilli, we had joint epiphanies. It started with a wish list on the back of a boarding pass; it ended with an oversized map freckled with Post-It notes.

Joy comes easily when you're away. It's not about beaches, boulevards, snow and city scapes, although they certainly help. It's the energy that comes with experiencing something new. It's an immediacy which makes it hard to think of anything else. There's also the anticipation. No matter how salty a day, having a trip on the horizon makes most things easier to swallow.

It wasn't long after that I dubbed the tall, blonde fellow, who later became my husband, 'The Hungry One'. It is a name borne as much from his appetite for life as his capacity to consume. Since that first adventure, he's passed some important lessons on to me. If you see a long queue for food, join it; locals will be waiting for a reason. I shared some tips of my own, gleaned the hard way after collecting *E. coli* from a local well in Malacca: just because it's washed, doesn't mean it's clean. But the most important thing we learnt was how to pack. Beyond a passport and a credit card, all we really needed was an open mind and an appetite.

Neither of us expected to find the world's best hot dogs in Iceland or a perfect schnitzel made by Austrian princes in Florence. As the years went on and a few curve balls were thrown our way, more Post-Its found their way onto the maps. From our base in Sydney we'd squelch our annual leave into a bundle and fly off to explore other corners of the world.

Later, after cramming clothes, books and a trusty red spatula into two suitcases, London became home. Weekend minibreaks, with cheap flights and a rush for seats in cattle class, were the order of the day. We'd leave on Friday night and eat and explore a city all weekend.

Many of the dishes in this book evolved from those trips. There were escapist lunches of garlic prawns with a pitcher of sangria in Estoril, and *pastillas* from the cool shadows of a Marrakech riad. Others came from more sobering places. We didn't intend to witness revolution when we went to the Great

Pyramids. Now when we eat *koshary*, we taste the adrenaline of people calling for freedom.

Nothing can transport me back to a place like a taste. A sip of Campari and I'm looking over Piazza San Marco. A glass of salmon-pink wine, beaded with sweat, and I'm watching boats nod in Menton. Put a Victoria beer in my hand and it will whisk me straight to Baja. More than a photo, a journal entry or a pair of souvenir cufflinks, it's the food that keeps the journeys alive. As long as I've got access to a kitchen and some inspiration I could be anywhere, and it's on those nights that I find I'm happier than ever to be home. I hope it works the same for you. *Bon voyage*.

POST CARD

THE ADDRESS TO BE WRITTEN ON THIS SIDE

Off to a good start

FOOD FOR A SOCIABLE START TO THE DAY
& WHEN YOU CRAVE BREAKFAST FOR DINNER

LONDON

The first time I visited London, the days were grey and the sky buckled like wet socks. It wasn't until I returned eight years later and tasted the mushrooms on toast at St. John restaurant that I began to properly chew on the prospect of uprooting our lives to live here. It's funny how a dish can do that. It might have been the resilient way the char of the bread held up against the sag of mushrooms. It might have been the hum of parsley and garlic. Whatever it was, over a plate of mushrooms on toast my resolve melted. This was not just a dish that made me feel at home. It was steadying enough to get me to contemplate shifting ours.

My recipe is not a replica of Fergus Henderson's mushrooms on toast. Those wanting the true experience should go to St. John in Smithfield, London, right now. This is the version I make when I can't get there. It serves as brunch, lunch or supper when I need an edible hug. The way the juices of the fungi soften the toast in the centre is a high point. For extra interest there's Parmesan, sage and burnt butter. My husband likes it with more bells and whistles. He'll happily pair it with prosciutto or a poached egg – or both. But to me the real heroes are the mushrooms. They work equally well over soft polenta, pasta or even puréed white beans for supper if you have a craving for mushrooms but just can't bring yourself to serve toast for dinner.

MUSHROOMS, BROWN BUTTER & PARMESAN ON TOAST

3 tablespoons butter
2 tablespoons olive oil
2 garlic cloves
1½ tablespoons sage leaves, half finely chopped, half kept whole
2 tablespoons flat leaf parsley leaves, finely chopped

400 g/14 oz. mixed mushrooms, sliced
3 tablespoons milk
1 handful Parmesan shavings
2 large slices of sourdough bread
salt and pepper

Serves 2

Melt 2 tablespoons of the butter in a large frying pan with the olive oil.

Cut 1 of the garlic cloves into slivers. Add it to the pan along with the chopped sage, half the parsley and a good pinch of salt. Swirl the pan over medium heat for 2 minutes to infuse the butter/oil.

Turn the heat up high and add the mushrooms, using tongs to toss them in the infused butter/oil.

When the mushrooms have browned and wilted, add the milk. Taste and season with salt and pepper.

Grill/broil the sourdough until lightly charred around the edges. Cut the remaining garlic clove in half and swipe it over the hot toast.

Divide the Parmesan between the slices of toast and scatter half the mushrooms and their juices over the top.

Return the empty frying pan to the heat. Add the remaining butter and sage and heat over medium heat until the sage is crisp and the butter has turned golden brown.

Drizzle the brown butter and crisp sage leaves over the mushrooms and toast. Serve hot.

To double this recipe for a crowd, you will have to use 2 frying pans: if you crowd the mushrooms, they will stew instead of brown and you don't want that.

NEW YORK

Introducing: the popover. You could think of it as the Yankee cousin of a Brit's Yorkshire pudding. It sits in the food family tree halfway between frittatas and crêpes, and resembles a souffléd muffin. The name 'popover' captures the way they creep and slump beyond their cooking case. The outside of a popover is crisp like toast, the interior soft. It's the perfect food for the city that never sleeps; not quite breakfast and not quite lunch, it also squats very happily on a dinner table next to Slow-cooked Pork Ribs (page 85). I first met popovers two blocks west of Central Park. They were plain. We smothered them with butter, ready blended with strawberry jam ('strawberry butter'!). These at-home versions take a savoury route, playing host to corn and punched up with chilli. For an amplified taste of New York, dress them with cream cheese and lox (cured salmon). Though in a city where excess is applauded, it's hard to go past lemon cream cheese and a sticky tomato relish bolstered with bacon.

CORN POPOVERS WITH TOMATO–BACON RELISH

Tomato-bacon relish
1 tablespoon olive oil
120 g/4 oz. lardons, streaky bacon or thick bacon, diced
1 red onion, cut into slim half moons
225 g/8 oz. cherry tomatoes, halved
1 tablespoon muscovado or brown sugar
2 tablespoons balsamic vinegar

To serve
150 g/⅔ cup cream cheese topped with 1 teaspoon lemon zest and a grinding of black pepper

Corn popovers
70 g/½ cup corn, lightly mashed with a fork (fresh, canned or frozen)
1 tablespoon butter, melted and cooled to room temperature, plus extra for greasing
130 g/1 cup plain/ all-purpose flour
1 teaspoon sugar
½ teaspoon salt
250 ml/1 cup milk
4 eggs, lightly beaten
1 teaspoon chilli powder
salt and black pepper

12-hole, non-stick popover or muffin pan

Makes 12 popovers

To make the tomato-bacon relish, heat the oil in a large saucepan and sauté the bacon and onion until the bacon fat has softened. Add the tomatoes, sugar and vinegar and cook over medium heat for 30–45 minutes until the tomatoes have wilted and the relish is jammy.

To make the corn popovers, if using frozen corn, defrost it in a frying pan with the melted butter. If using fresh or canned corn, simply mix it with the melted butter.

In a bowl, mix together the flour, sugar, salt and a grinding of pepper.

Stir in the milk, eggs, and butter and corn mixture until evenly combined. Allow the batter to rest for 30 minutes.

Preheat the oven to 230°C (450°F) Gas 8 and put the popover/muffin pan inside to heat up.

Remove the hot pan from the oven and carefully grease the holes with extra butter. Pour the batter into each hole until it comes three-quarters of the way up.

Bake in the oven for 25 minutes or until puffed and golden. Serve straight from the oven with the tomato-bacon relish and cream cheese.

Feel free to substitute peas for the corn.

COCONUT, LIME & GINGER TAPIOCA WITH LYCHEES & TOASTED COCONUT

2-cm/1-inch piece of fresh ginger, roughly chopped
zest of 1 lime, in 1 piece
250 ml/1 cup milk
100 g/½ cup (caster) sugar
75 g/½ cup small pearl tapioca (not quick-cooking)

1 x 400-ml/14-oz. can unsweetened coconut milk

To serve
120 g/1 cup peeled lychees, fresh or canned
juice of 1 lime
20 g/½ cup coconut flakes

Serves 6

PHI PHI ISLAND

Some days you need to pretend you're in Thailand. Over four days on Phi Phi Island we ate our body weight in banana pancakes and tapioca puddings. We loved that place.

When I need sunshine, these are the flavours I turn to: ginger wakes me up, coconut makes me look for palm trees and lime makes my palms itch for a cocktail, preferably with a novelty umbrella.

Tapioca must be one of the most soothing substances around. The little pearls, like bean-bag stuffing, are available from most Asian food stores. With some coaxing, they swell into cuddly spheres suspended in a custard-style sauce.

Eaten hot or cold, it's perfect after Asian-spiced fish or an aromatic meat like duck, or as part of a breakfast banquet with a big platter of fruit salad.

I like to eat it while listening to bad pop music and wearing fisherman's trousers that seemed like a good idea at the time. That way I really feel like I'm on holiday.

Put 250 ml/1 cup water in a saucepan with the ginger and lime zest and bring to the boil. Once it's come to the boil, cover with a lid and remove from the heat. Allow to steep for 20 minutes.

Fish the ginger and lime out of the water. Put back on the heat, add the milk, sugar, tapioca and coconut milk and bring to the boil over high heat.

Once boiled, reduce the heat to medium and simmer for 20–30 minutes, stirring occasionally with a metal spoon to prevent it sticking to the bottom of the pan. Cook until all the liquid has been absorbed and the tapioca has thickened to the texture of a droopy porridge. Transfer to bowls.

Serve warm or chilled, but just before serving, toast the coconut flakes in a dry frying pan until they brown at the edges.

If using fresh lychees, peel and stone/pit them and cut them into quarters. Dress them with the lime juice. Top the bowls of pudding with the lychees and toasted coconut.

Coconut flakes are different from desiccated coconut – they're wafts of coconut flesh that toast beautifully. If you can't get them, substitute with toasted flaked/slivered almonds.

PARIS

Paris played host to our honeymoon. We spent our mornings eating pâtisserie and shovelling fresh berries from the rue Mouffetard market into our mouths while squinting at rotating maps in an effort to orient ourselves. We got lost and meandered over cobbled streets, gazing moonily in real-estate windows, dreaming of an alternate reality in which I would wear hats at rakish angles and speak French fluently. Those fictions stayed in Paris, but this pudding came back with us. It's at home both on a breakfast table with yogurt and at the close of an evening meal with puddles of ice cream or cream. The croissants channel an English bread pudding into France, yet you could easily substitute brioche, pannetone or a supermarket loaf. To feel like you're in my Paris, just mangle your vocabulary at the boulangerie, then be too embarrassed to say you wanted two croissants, not twelve. When you get home with more than you can possibly eat, you can put some of the excess to good use here, while you toil a little harder on your pronunciation.

RASPBERRY CROISSANT PUDDING

1 tablespoon butter
2 eggs plus 3 egg yolks
1 teaspoon vanilla
    extract
475 ml/2 cups milk
100 g/½ cup (caster)
    sugar
6 croissants, preferably
    stale
150 g/1 cup raspberries
    (if frozen, let them
    defrost and the juices
    strain), plus a few
    extra to serve

six 250-ml/1-cup ramekins
deep baking pan

Serves 6

Preheat the oven to 180°C (350°F) Gas 4. Grease the ramekins with butter.

Whisk the eggs, egg yolks, vanilla, milk and sugar together. Tear the croissants into pieces the size of a matchbook. Place half the croissants across the bottom of the ramekins. Add the raspberries, then the remaining croissants.

Pour the custard over the croissants and allow to soak for 10 minutes.

Cover each ramekin with foil and puncture the top to let the steam escape. Try not to let the foil touch the mixture.

Put the ramekins in a deep baking pan. Pour hot water into the pan until it comes halfway up the sides of the ramekins. Bake for 40 minutes or until the custard is set. Serve warm with more fresh raspberries.

SYDNEY **When the sun is out and the day is clear, it's easy for a Sydney brunch to slip into beers, a walk and then dinner with friends by the coast.** This is a dish built for that sort of weekend. Fritters hold their own both on a breakfast table and later on if someone fires up a barbecue. My preferred way to eat them is in the morning with squashed roasted tomatoes and prosciutto, but a dipping sauce of yogurt muddled with basil and mint or an avocado purée are also worth thinking about. If the weekend gets a touch too exciting and your original plans go completely awry, they also freeze well and can be happily warmed in the oven or a toasted sandwich maker.

PEA, BASIL & FETA FRITTERS WITH ROASTED TOMATOES

Roasted tomatoes
300 g/2 cups cherry
    tomatoes, halved
2 tablespoons olive oil
2 tablespoons balsamic
    vinegar

Fritters
200 g/1⅓ cups frozen
    peas, quickly defrosted
    (you can use the
    pan you'll fry the
    fritters in)
100 g/¾ cup plain/
    all-purpose flour
1 teaspoon baking
    powder

1 egg
150 ml/⅔ cup milk
grated zest of ½ lemon
100 g/⅔ cup crumbled
    feta cheese
30 basil leaves, torn into
    small shreds
2 tablespoons olive oil
salt and black pepper

To serve
100 g/3½ oz. prosciutto

Makes 12–14 fritters,
or serves 4 for brunch

Preheat the oven to 180°C (350°F) Gas 4.

For the roasted tomatoes, put the halved cherry tomatoes on a baking sheet, drizzle with the olive oil and vinegar and sprinkle with a few pinches of salt. Roast in the oven for 25–35 minutes until the tomatoes are lightly caramelized.

For the fritters, lightly defrost the peas over medium heat in a frying pan.

Combine the flour, baking powder, egg, milk and lemon zest in a mixing bowl. Stir in the crumbled feta, torn basil and warmed peas. Season with salt and pepper.

Heat 1 tablespoon of the olive oil in the frying pan. Spoon 1½ tablespoons of batter per fritter into the hot pan. Cook 3 fritters at a time over medium heat until you see small holes appearing on the surface. Gently flip with a spatula and cook for 2 minutes on the other side. Transfer to somewhere warm while you make the rest.

Serve the fritters with the roasted tomatoes and prosciutto. A few extra basil leaves or baby spinach leaves would also be nice.

Substitute mint or parsley for basil and goats' cheese, torn mozzarella or halloumi for the feta.

HOW TO GET THE BEST OUT OF A BREAKFAST BUFFET

Making the most of a breakfast buffet is both an art and a science. Some people are very good at this; others really aren't.

To really tackle a hotel buffet requires a proper strategy. Here are some tips I've picked up along the way.

Step 1: Don't falter on the edge of the forest like Bambi.

It's all about making a plan. Get to know your terrain. Even if it's your second or third morning at the hotel, a casual lap or two around the buffet will help you scope it out – just in case it changes day to day.

Where are the pastries? Where is the yogurt? Where is the juice? What's the special? Where have they tucked the delightful fellow flipping the omelettes? And most importantly – how far away is that station from the toaster?

Step 2: Take the time to investigate the beverage options.

I've learnt (the sad way) not to assume that you'll be limited to tepid tea and bitter coffee. There could be espressos and banana smoothies. There could be freshly squeezed spirulina and pineapple frappés. There could be hot chocolate with tiny marshmallows bobbing about – and you could be missing it all.

Step 3: Formulate a deployment strategy.

The aim of each trip back to the buffet is to construct complete plates out of what's available. But it's important to keep some sense. Ask yourself questions. Would I normally have baked beans with a sticky praline pastry? Would I normally have a side of watermelon snuggling up to my sausages? Probably not. These things are not usually friends on a plate.

Step 4: Make a savoury plate.

Pick your eggs. You can usually judge the standard of any hotel buffet by their poached proteins and whether they'll do them to order. If the egg comes in a little metal collar, I walk away. That's what McHappy day is for.

But if they're making eggs to order, get two eggs poaching and use the three minutes you now have up your sleeve to source some carbohydrates. I'll go and put my bread in the funny little toaster conveyor belt. I sniff out the smoked salmon in the strangely Scandinavian cold-meat section. I start to source out the cheese board; I'll probably find the cream cheese hiding in the back. I locate some grilled/broiled tomatoes from the bain marie. I grab my toast. Grab my eggs. Then I make a plate.

Suddenly I'm looking down at a first course of poached eggs on a cream cheese and smoked salmon bagel with a side of roasted tomato.

A similar principle applies to pairing omelettes with baked beans, mushrooms and hash browns. There, a real cooked breakfast. I made it myself. Sort of.

Step 5: Sort out your sweet carbohydrates.

Throughout all of this there's a question I want to keep running through my head: 'If this was on a menu, would I order it?'

If what's on my plate starts to read like a listing of 'pancakes, french toast, hash browns, grapefruit and a tub of yogurt with a last-minute glugging of maple syrup', I know I've lost the plot and the point of the exercise.

In some of the best cases I could have bircher muesli, yogurt and fruit.

But stop – are there some flaked almonds over with the cheese I could add to the top? Could some berry coulis that was meant for the pancakes be swirled through it to take it to the next level?

Or could I be finding some coconut bread and top that with a banana I've sliced, some fruit purée or a dollop of vanilla yogurt and raisins?

Step 6: Get a fruit plate going.

Fruit is nice at breakfast. Put a little

yogurt on the side. Find the honey in the condiment section. Then dip the fruit in it. Now it's even better.

Step 7: Stay the course. And get a fresh plate.

It's important not to get too pleased with yourself and go crazy at this point. If I haven't committed at the start to an Asian-themed breakfast, I've learnt not to suddenly think dim sum and congee are going to be a good addition to the journey. Instead it's time to nibble on a pastry while I finish my coffee. A fresh plate is important. The last thing you want is a croissant glugging about in a sticky river of pink watermelon sludge.

Step 8: Confirm your exit strategy.

Then it's time for the final hurdle – smuggling an apple, a muffin and a couple of rolls into my handbag so there's something for lunch.

Because in this battle, the true victor is decided not by how much you've eaten for breakfast, but by how little you need to buy for lunch.

AGADIR

After six months of an extended London winter, we were as bland as egg whites.

Come Easter we ran to the orange sands of Morocco. The coast of Agadir has real surf; one dunk in the waters and we were reborn. These eggs may not have been the traditional pink-hued shells from our childhood holidays, but they served us well for brunch on Good Friday. Over a base of spiced and stewed peppers, onions and carrots, we placed poached eggs. We chased after their streaking yolks with puffed breads. Baked eggs are less of a fuss than poaching. These ones still carry a good kick of life. The cumin brings some dark murkiness to the table and the chilli sings of warmth. The best thing is that these eggs don't require your full attention. Make the spiced ratatouille base and crack the eggs on top (don't break the yolk). Give the yolks a bonnet of yogurt and garlic, then leave them be. Go surfing. Go walking. Spend time with loved ones. All they need is 16 minutes in the oven and a sprinkling of salt and pepper, or a dash of chilli sauce. The yolks will bleed into the base like sunset over sand. Every time I eat them, these eggs transport me straight to a place where it's warm. I hope they do the same for you.

BAKED MOROCCAN EGGS

1½ teaspoons ground cumin

1 tablespoon olive oil

1 onion, cut into thin half moons

1 carrot, grated

1 teaspoon chopped red chilli

1 red pepper, cut into 1-cm/½-inch strips

1 yellow pepper, cut into 1-cm/½-inch strips

2 teaspoons salt

2 eggs

2 tablespoons natural yogurt

1 garlic clove, grated

toasted pita bread, to serve

two 250-ml1-cup ramekins

Serves 2

Preheat the oven to 180°C (350°F) Gas 4.

Toast the cumin in a dry frying pan for 30 seconds until it smells nutty. Add the olive oil and onion. Sauté the onion until it is translucent.

Add the grated carrot, chilli and strips of pepper. Sauté for 5 minutes until the peppers have softened their hard edges.

Add 120 ml/½ cup water and turn the heat down to medium. Continue to cook for about 15 minutes until the peppers and onions have relaxed into a gentle compote. You should end up with 250–350 ml/1–1½ cups compote. Season well with salt.

Divide the compote into 2 ramekins, making sure there's at least 2 cm/¾ inch clear at the top of the ramekin. Create a well in the centre of the compote with the back of a spoon. Crack an egg over the top of the peppers. Don't allow the yolk to break.

Float a tablespoon of yogurt over each egg yolk. Sprinkle half a teaspoon of grated garlic over the yogurt. Bake for 16 minutes, until the whites are set, but the yolk is still runny.

Serve with toasted pita bread.

You can also make this with stewed aubergine/ eggplant, roasted tomatoes or caponata (page 133) as a base.

MADRID

It's all about the ham. Some people may go for flamenco, others to sticky-beak at the bull fighting. But for a real taste of Madrid, you have to get stuck into the *jamón*. We reached the pinnacle of acorn-fed pig consumption at the Museo del Jamón on Calle Mayor. It's not really a museum, more a cafeteria crossed with a butcher or charcuterie store. Here's how it works. Stand at the bar. Marvel at the scores of hams hanging from the ceilings like fat, overlapping tiles. Choose something from the laminated sheets affixed to the mirrors on the walls. It's very hard to go past warm baguette with smushed tomato and layered with pieces of ham: *pan tumaca con Ibérico*. This recipe takes the formula of pairing tomato bread with *jamón* and gilds it further, with fried eggs and some sneaky chips/fries. For the ultimate indulgence, wrap one of the potato chips in ham and puncture the egg yolk with it. Then use the tomato bread to mop up the excess. If bliss has a taste, this could be it.

FRIED EGGS, TOMATO BREAD, JAMON & CHIPS

300 g/10 oz. floury
    potatoes
250 ml/1 cup sunflower
    or canola oil, for frying
2 tomatoes
2 garlic cloves
2 tablespoons good
    olive oil, plus extra
    for frying

2 eggs
4 slices of sourdough
    toast or toasted
    baguette
2 pinches salt
100 g/3½ oz. jamón
    Ibérico

Serves 2

Trim the potatoes into squarish shapes (don't bother to peel them). Cut into chips/fries 1 cm/¾ inch thick and dry well on kitchen paper.

Heat the sunflower oil in a deep pan or deep-fat fryer to 140°C (275°F). Make sure the oil is at least 3 cm/1¼ inches deep. Fry the chips for 4 minutes, then scoop out and drain on kitchen paper.

While the chips are frying, make the tomato bread. Grate the tomatoes through a sharp grater into a bowl. Some of the skin won't go through, but that's OK. You want a mushy pulp. Grate in 1 garlic clove. Whisk in 2 tablespoons olive oil and season with a good pinch of salt.

Dry the chips well on kitchen paper, turn up the heat to 180°C (350°F) and fry the chips for another 3–4 minutes until golden and crisp. Remove and dry on kitchen paper and season well with salt and pepper. Fry the eggs in a little olive oil until the whites are cooked and the yolks are still runny.

Toast 2 slices of thick sourdough or baguette.

Cut the remaining garlic clove in half and rub the cut side over the toast while it is still hot. Top with the tomato mush. Serve the chips, fried eggs and tomato bread with the jamón. Suggest that people wrap a chip in jamón, then use that to puncture the gooey yolks.

The tomato bread is also spectacular as a snack or starter/appetizer with a platter of cured meats.

MARATHON MILO BIRCHER MUESLI

250 ml/1 cup milk (any kind is fine. The Hungry One likes almond milk)

6 tablespoons Milo

200 g/1½ cups rolled/traditional oats

150 g/⅔ cup Greek yogurt

60 g/½ cup almonds and brazil nuts, toasted

2 bananas, thinly sliced

Serves 4, or 2 marathon runners

Mix together the milk and Milo. Put the oats in a large bowl and add the Milo milk. Stir and leave to soak overnight.

When ready to serve, add the yogurt. Stir and transfer to serving bowls. Top with the nuts and sliced bananas just before serving.

Milo is a powdered malt chocolate drink; others, like Ovaltine, can be substituted. Diced dates or prunes would be nice additions. It will keep in the fridge in a sealed container for a few days. It's good to have on hand for early-morning exercise, whether it's cycling, rowing, swimming or training to run very long distances.

MELBOURNE

The story goes that the first man to run a marathon arrived at his destination, then dropped dead. This is not a comforting tale to hear the night before your husband embarks on his first one. This malted chocolate bircher muesli was first made in a Tupperware container in a hotel room in Melbourne. All the beers from the minibar fridge were banished to make room for it. The muesli was full of good things for serious exercise: oats, malt, nuts and bananas for extra get-up-and-go. The next morning The Hungry One pinned a number to his chest, stretched his calves, put Vaseline in his pocket and ran from the Melbourne Cricket Ground, out along the windswept bay of St Kilda and back into the city. I dashed from spot to spot, trying to find him in a crowd. I held out lurid drinks pimped with electrolytes to him and other tall blondes that resembled him at a distance. Towards the end I started bleating strange things I thought might motivate him, like 'there's a boutique back at the hotel!' That morning I'd gone out and re-stocked the minibar with things I knew he liked to drink. Later, back in the room with his swollen feet up, he declined the booze but asked if there was any muesli left. There wasn't. Wouldn't you know it, this time I'd sacrificed the bircher to make room for the beer. We live and learn.

SYDNEY

A cup of coffee and a slice of banana bread. How many mornings have been made by this coupling? Yet the days when you crave it are so often the ones when it's hardest to cleave out the time. So, in a spirit of efficiency, here the two components come together as one.

This loaf's appeal doesn't just lie in how the coffee tempers the candy sweetness of ripe bananas, plumbing it with a note of caramel. (Overly ripe bananas plucked from the pit of the freezer are best – you might as well use cooked parsnip for all the flavour green bananas will bring.) It's not just about how the milky coffee keeps the bread moist and cake-like (let's not kid ourselves, this is cake, even if we eat it in the morning). This is about making your breakfast work harder for you. You're probably multi-tasking all day long, and I don't think it's too much to expect a piece of cake to put in a similar effort.

Surrounded by pubs, yoga studios, eclectic furniture stores and a performing arts school, breakfast out in Newtown, in Sydney's inner west, was traditionally driven by two factors. I'd either be dusty from time spent in one of the local pubs or smug after an early class working through the asanas. This Berocca frappé works equally well in both contexts. There's a slight fizz from the Berocca; the pineapple juice and mint are zesty enough to lift you out of a concrete jungle and transport you to somewhere tropical; and the banana gives it ballast. You could add some blueberries if you want. It's a frappé best drunk soon after making. Then go and do another yoga class. Buy a divan you'll later regret. Or go back to bed.

LATTE BANANA BREAD

110 g/7 tablespoons soft butter
300 g/2⅓ cups plain/all-purpose flour
1 teaspoon bicarbonate of soda/baking soda
1 teaspoon salt
125 g/⅔ cup sugar
2 eggs
4 ripe bananas, mashed
85 ml/⅓ cup milky coffee (1 shot of espresso topped up with milk)

20 x 12.5-cm/8 x 5-inch loaf pan, greased

Serves 6–8

Preheat the oven to 180°C (350°F) Gas 4.

Sift the flour, bicarbonate of soda/baking soda and salt into a large mixing bowl.

In a separate bowl, use a hand mixer to beat the butter and sugar together until light and fluffy.

Add the eggs, mashed bananas and coffee to the butter and sugar mixture and stir well. Fold in the flour mixture. Do this gently; you don't want to overwork the flour and have it turn out tough.

Tip the mixture into the prepared loaf pan. Bake in the preheated oven for about 1 hour, or until well risen and golden brown.

Remove from the oven and allow to cool in the pan for a few minutes, then turn out onto a wire rack to cool further before serving.

Serve with a coffee on the side. Perhaps with some ricotta or butter over the top.

BEROCCA FRAPPE

**1 Berocca/fizzing
  multivitamin tablet
250 ml/1 cup pineapple
  juice
1 banana
12 mint leaves**

*jug blender or stick
blender*

Serves 1

Let the Berocca tablet
fizz away in 120 ml/
½ cup cold water. Add
the pineapple juice,
banana and mint leaves.
    Blend until smooth
and frothy.

BONDI

'You only live once.' These words are ghost-written on the glass wall of a North Bondi Italian at the far end of Sydney's most iconic beach. If that's true, then nursing a Campari on ice while picking at a platter of griddled bread with ricotta, mint, chilli and lemon is not a bad way to do it. This is a perfect light lunch or appetizer for a group – though you could also bust it out for breakfast (perhaps leave the Campari for later). For the true Bondi bruschetta experience, emerge from the surf 10 minutes prior to eating, with sand still plastered to places you can't quite see. It's best to secure a good char on the edges of the bread to contrast with the pale plume of ricotta. The rest is relatively simple; the mint leaves need to be spanking fresh and you want enough dried chilli, salt and pepper on the table so that everyone can build their own combinations. Start with ricotta, then layer up torn mint, lemon juice, chilli flakes and pepper. Salt is essential to make it sparkle. If some of it is what's stowed away on your fingertips after a long swim in the surf, that's more than OK.

GRIDDLED BREAD WITH RICOTTA, MINT, CHILLI & LEMON

4 slices of good
    sourdough bread
2 tablespoons good
    olive oil
100 g/½ cup good
    ricotta cheese
1 tablespoon dried chilli
    flakes
1 lemon
20 mint leaves, torn
flaky salt and black
    pepper

ridged grill pan

Serves 4

Drizzle each slice of bread with the olive oil and griddle it on the ridged grill pan until lightly charred.

Put the ricotta in a bowl and top with the dried chilli and grated zest of half the lemon.

Serve the bread and ricotta on a platter with the mint leaves, lemon wedges and salt and pepper on the side.

Encourage people to make their own bruschettas with chilli, ricotta, mint leaves and lemon juice, and plenty of salt and pepper.

WAILEA

You won't spy many pupu platters in Wailea without poke.

Wailea is a jewel of Maui, a beach suburb populated by giant turtles and wealthy folk gadding about in golf carts. It's also where beautiful people (not us) go to get married. *Pupus* are the protein-heavy snacks visitors pick at while the sun stains the sky cerise and bridal parties pose for photographs. *Poke* (pronounced *poh-kay*) means 'a small piece'. The traditional versions are a mix of raw fish, salt, seaweed and inamona nuts. Most of the renditions we scoffed involved diced raw ahi tuna, garnished with sesame seeds, spring onions/scallions and avocado. A little bit of chilli keeps things sprightly. At home I serve them in lettuce cups or on cucumber coins. I make it while listening to 'IZ' Ka'ano'i Kamakawiwo'ole's version of *Over the Rainbow*, as if I were the first person to clock its ability to transport me straight back to paradise. Tucking a flower behind your ear while you serve is optional (though potentially overkill).

POKE

600 g/1 lb. 5 oz. fresh or sashimi-grade fish (tuna is classic, but to avoid eating over-fished tuna, you can substitute any other sashimi-grade fish)
½ teaspoon sugar
3 tablespoons soy sauce
1 tablespoon sesame oil
1 tablespoon grated fresh ginger
1 tablespoon finely chopped red chilli
35 g/½ cup (about 5) chopped spring onions/scallions
1 tablespoon black sesame seeds
1 tablespoon white sesame seeds

1 large avocado, diced into 1-cm/½-inch dice
1 head iceberg lettuce, or thick cucumber slices, slightly hollowed out, to serve

Serves 6–8 as a starter/appetizer or light meal with sticky rice

Trim any sinew or bloodlines off the fish. Cut the flesh into 1-cm/¾-inch dice.

Stir the sugar into the soy sauce until it dissolves. Mix with the sesame oil, ginger and chilli. Combine the soy dressing with the fish. Gently fold through the spring onions/scallions, sesame seeds and avocado.

Serve with lettuce leaves to wrap around or pile onto thick slices of cucumber.

To make this heartier, serve with warm sticky rice made just before serving.

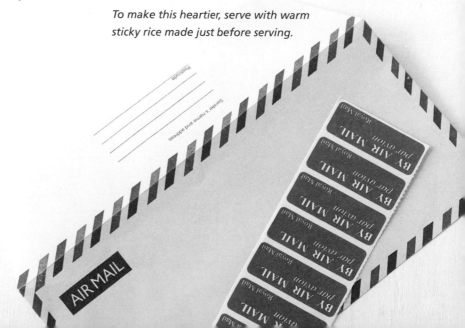

POST CARD

1ST

NADI

In the languor of days, when the most taxing activities are replying 'bula' to boundless friendly greetings and recovering from the trauma of wearing paper pants to a massage, cooking is sometimes not an option. Yes, our Fijian bungalow had a barbecue. We could grill fresh fish to our hearts' content while looking at the freakishly turquoise water. Yet all we wanted to do was babysit cold beers and eat bowls of this. *Kokoda* is a coconut ceviche that's popular in the Pacific. The fish is 'cooked' by the citrus, then softened by the coconut milk. There's chilli for warmth and tomato and onion for freshness. Like the *poke* (previous page), at home I like to serve it in lettuce cups for a light, low-carbohydrate dinner. If there's a crowd, I often put all the elements on a platter so people can mix their own. This is best eaten while sipping a Fiji Bitter and watching out for turtles burying their eggs in the sand.

KOKODA

250 g/8 oz. fresh mahi-mahi, snapper or sea bass, skinned and pin-boned

juice of 1 lime

2 spring onions/scallions, sliced

½ green chilli, thinly sliced

1 Roma tomato, seeds removed, chopped into small dice

90 ml/⅓ cup coconut milk

1 head iceberg or romaine lettuce

salt

Serves 4 as a starter/appetizer or light meal

Cut the fish into 1-cm/¾-inch dice and sprinkle with salt. Add the lime juice and stir thoroughly so that the lime juice 'cooks' the fish. Cover and marinate for 30 minutes in the fridge.

Toss the fish, then return to the fridge for another 30 minutes.

Combine the fish with the spring onions/scallions, chilli and tomato. Strain off some of the juices that will have gathered at the bottom.

Transfer to a bowl and pour the coconut milk over the top.

Serve with lettuce leaves to wrap the fish in.

PISMO BEACH

Every year the elephant seals come ashore at Piedras Blancas on the Californian coast. They lumber across the sand with the sort of pace you'd expect for something that weighs more than 1,500 kilograms (3,300 pounds) and is propelled by flippers.

The alpha males have beards of flesh which drape from their noses and are flanked by scores of females. Meanwhile the B-grade bulls form the outer ring of the colony, happy to take what they can get. It's a little like a high-school dance. Except what they get up to on the sand was not permitted at any dance I attended.

An hour down the coast, the sands of Pismo Beach are more peaceful. There's a long pier to walk along while you reconcile what you've just seen. And then there's the cracked crab. There's not much that's civilized about this way of eating. First, you need to put on a bib. Then a toy hammer will be placed in your hand. Soon a bucket of cooked crab and potato will be dumped on the table for you to plough through with your hands. It's a good way to nurture your inner child after seeing some fairly adult things.

At home, this is a solid way to entertain a crowd. Put butcher's paper on a long table outside. Get folks to BYO beer and hammers. Make sturdy servings of aïoli, both plain and spiked with chilli. Cook some sausages and potatoes. Perhaps some ears of corns. Dump the food along the butcher's paper for everyone to fossick through. Come up for air when the table is pure carnage and your stomachs are as round as a pregnant elephant seal.

SMASHED CRAB, SAUSAGE & POTATOES WITH AÏOLI

6 medium live crabs
8 spicy pork sausages
6 medium roasting potatoes
1 recipe Aïoli (page 57)
4 lemons

hammers and a large baking sheet

Serves 6

Put the crabs in the freezer for 30 minutes before you cook them.

Preheat the oven to 180°C (350°F) Gas 4. Put the potatoes in a large pot of cold salted water with a lemon, cut in half, and bring to the boil. Continue to cook at a rolling boil for 5 minutes, then fish the potatoes out of the water, cut into quarters and put on a large baking sheet. Drizzle with olive oil and salt and bake for 30 minutes.

Top up the potato/lemon water, bring to the boil and boil the crabs in batches. There should be enough water so the crabs are submerged, plus another 10 cm/4 inches of water on top of that. Boil the crabs for 15 minutes.

After the potatoes have baked for 30 minutes, add the sausages to the baking sheet and continue to cook for 20 minutes, or until the potatoes and sausages are crisp.

Put some clean butcher's paper down the centre of a table. Put the crabs, potato and sausage in a pile in the centre with the aïoli on the side. Give everyone a hammer and half a lemon to squeeze over.

Crack open the crabs, eat with your hands, dipping pieces of sausage, potato and crab in the aïoli. Make a glorious mess.

The lemon in the water will help add a gentle flavour to the potatoes. You could also substitute a lime or a clementine for something different. Make a few aïolis, one aggressively flavoured with lemon zest and another with chilli. Smoked paprika or parsley aïoli would also be nice.

AVOCA BEACH

Just as there are sounds that whisk us to memories, there are tastes that transport me straight to a place.

This pulled pork with pineapple salsa is one of them. I rarely make it when I'm not at Avoca, an hour and a half north of Sydney; a small town with a long, smiling curve of a beach. At one end is a rockpool. The rest is a mix of galumphing waves and a tepid lagoon.

Avoca is where we went for the weddings of our best friends and weekend breaks. Avoca was where we ran after The Hungry One's mum was taken from him. Two days after spending time in the grey light of Paddington police station, we drove fiercely towards the sand, tight embraces and the hope that the salt on our faces would soon come from the surf.

It was 12 months later that I first made this salsa. We were feeding 15 at a long table balanced on ankle-length grass overlooking the sea. Beyond the slow-cooked pork, there was a big pot of beans and enough guacamole to feed an army. By our feet were beach buckets filled with Coronas and ice and the fixings for home-made fireworks.

This salsa is sweet and spicy, a chaotic tumble of fun. It's best eaten with pulled pork that's been braised in pineapple juice and beer while watching Catherine wheels pop over the sand.

PORK BURRITOS WITH SPICY PINEAPPLE SALSA

Spicy pineapple salsa
½ pineapple
½ red onion, finely diced
juice and grated zest of
    1 lime
1 small bunch coriander/
    cilantro
1 tablespoon jalapeños
    from a jar, diced
1 fresh jalapeño or other
    green chilli, diced

Pulled pork
zest of 1 small orange
1 tablespoon ground
    cumin
½ tablespoon sea salt
1 teaspoon ground
    coriander
½ teaspoon black pepper
½ teaspoon chilli powder
1 kg/2¼ lbs. well-marbled
    pork shoulder/butt,

roughly chopped
1 tablespoon olive oil
120 ml/½ cup pineapple
    juice
350 ml/12 fl. oz. Corona
    or other Mexican beer
1 bay leaf
2 tablespoons pumpkin
    seeds/pepitas

To serve
flour tortillas
½ white cabbage,
    shredded
hot sauce, to taste
1 recipe Guacamole
    (page 45)
60 g/2 oz. mozzarella,
    cubed
60 g/2 oz. goats' cheese,
    crumbled

Serves 4–6

Spicy pineapple salsa
Cut the skin off the pineapple, quarter it and cut into small cubes. Combine it with the red onion, lime zest and juice. Finely chop the coriander/cilantro stems and add to the bowl. Add both types of jalapeño, including the seeds if you want it hot. Stir to combine. Add the coriander/cilantro leaves just before serving.

Pulled pork
Mix together the spices, salt, pepper and orange zest. Dust the pork in the spices. Heat the olive oil in a casserole dish over high heat. Brown the meat in 2 batches. Return all the meat to the pan and pour the pineapple juice and beer on top. Top up with enough water to just cover the meat. Add the bay leaf. Bring the pork and liquid to a rolling boil, then reduce the heat to a simmer and cook, uncovered, for 2 hours.

Check the meat and continue cooking until there is only 5 mm/¼ inch of liquid left in the pot and the meat easily shreds with 2 forks. 2½ hours should do it.

Allow to rest for 10 minutes. Shred the meat with 2 forks and toss it with the remaining juices.

Top the pork with the pumpkin seeds before serving with flour tortillas, pineapple salsa, shredded white cabbage, hot sauce, guacamole and cheese.

BAJA
(TO ATTEMPT TO LEARN TO SURF)

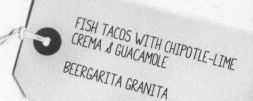

FISH TACOS WITH CHIPOTLE-LIME CREMA & GUACAMOLE

BEERGARITA GRANITA

I discovered a taste for beer while attempting to surf in Baja. Corona may be one of the best-known Mexican lagers, but Victoria was my favourite, and not just for the novelty of being able to point at the *casita* and say, 'I think there's a beer up there with my name on it'.

During a week in a dusty surf camp four hours south of San Diego, these are some things I learnt. 1) Falling off the rear of a wave feels like running for a bus and having the doors close in your face. 2) It's important to be able to carry your own stuff. 3) The best way to check if the fish tacos in Ensenada are safe to eat is if the *crema* bottles have condensation on them (condensation means proper refrigeration, which means less likelihood of Montezuma's Revenge). Meanwhile, our instructor learnt he should never, ever blow a horn at an Australian surfing while there are seals cavorting nearby. The Australian will scan expectantly for teeth and a fin, then paddle towards the shore very fast.

After catching two waves, missing eleven, wiping out twice, escaping from fictional sharks, wrestling limbs from the vacuum suck of a full steamer and carrying an eight-foot board over jagged rocks, you'll probably deserve a drink. This is a feast that justifies the purchase of some Mexican lager, not just because they're a good match, but because you'll need one for dessert.

A true Baja fish taco boasts a crispy carapace of fried batter that protects flakes of white fish. There's earthiness from the corn tortilla and a pale and bitter crunch in the shredded cabbage. Then there's the sniffing, sour burn of Tapatio chilli sauce. This version takes the original concept and makes it a little more wetsuit friendly. Instead of frying the fish, it's roasted with a gentle crust of coriander/cilantro leaves and pumpkin seeds. What you miss in fatty crunch is made up for by the winning addition of guacamole and chipotle-lime crema. It's the taste of summer. It's the smell of success, even if you are getting dumped more often than you're standing tall.

The beergarita is an excellent dessert for a Mexican feast and a barometer of how much booze you've consumed. The sour notes of the beer hang five against the citrus tang of the lime, tequila brings warmth and ice shards cool you down. But if you can't manage to say 'Beergarita Granita' twice, and fast, by the time dessert rolls around, you probably shouldn't be having any.

FISH TACOS WITH CHIPOTLE-LIME CREMA

Chipotle-lime crema
1 dried chipotle chilli plus 2 tablespoons just-boiled water (or substitute chipotle powder, or smoked barbecue sauce with cayenne pepper)
4 tablespoons crème fraîche, sour cream or natural yogurt
juice and zest of ½ lime
a few coriander/ cilantro leaves

Fish tacos
700 g/1 lb. 9 oz. skinless white fish fillets (such as sea bass, John Dory, barramundi or mahi-mahi)

2 handfuls coriander/ cilantro leaves and stems, chopped
1 handful pumpkin seeds/pepitas
2 tablespoons olive oil
zest of ½ lime

To serve
warmed corn or wheat soft tortillas or tacos (2–3 per person)
4 large handfuls shredded white cabbage
jalapeños, to taste
salt

stick blender or small food processor

Serves 4

Chipotle-lime crema
Split the dried chipotle chilli and shake out most of the seeds. Dry-toast it in a frying pan until it smells nutty. Cover it with just-boiled water and steep for 15 minutes. Purée the chilli and the steeping water until smooth.

Put 2 teaspoons of the chipotle purée in the bottom of a blender. Add the crème fraîche and lime zest and juice. Process until smooth and top with a few coriander/cilantro leaves.

Fish tacos
Preheat the oven to 200°C (400°F) Gas 6.

Dry the fish fillets well and place them on a baking sheet. Cover them with a flurry of coriander leaves, pumpkin seeds, a drizzle of olive oil and the zest of half a lime (use the juice in the guacamole).

Bake the fish for 10–12 minutes, until the flesh is opaque, or wrap in foil and grill on the barbecue. Break each cooked fillet into thirds (keeping the pumpkin seeds and coriander with each one). Place the fish on a serving platter with the tortillas, guacamole, shredded cabbage, chipotle-lime crema and jalapeños, and assemble your own tacos.

Any remaining chipotle purée can be frozen in an ice cube tray, so there's some on hand next time you make tacos, burritos, enchiladas or pulled pork.

GUACAMOLE

2 ripe avocados
juice of ½ lime
1 handful coriander/cilantro
    leaves, roughly chopped
60 g/2 cups good corn chips,
    warmed in the oven for
    10 minutes
6 soft corn tortillas, wrapped
    in foil and warmed in the
    oven
salt

Halve the avocados and cut out any brown bits. Remove the stones/pits. Use a fork to scrape the avocado flesh from the skin.

Mash the avocado flesh with the lime juice, salt and half the coriander/cilantro. Top with the remaining coriander and a sprinkle of salt. Eat with warm corn chips and warm tortillas. For a textural riot, combine the two.

BEERGARITA GRANITA

Beergarita
300 g/1½ cups sugar
175 ml/⅔ cup fresh lime
    juice (about 6 limes)
zest of 2 limes
6 tablespoons triple sec
    or Cointreau
250 ml/1 cup Mexican
    beer (such as Corona,
    Victoria or Sol)
8 tablespoons tequila

Lime sugar rim
100 g/½ cup caster/
    superfine sugar
50 g/¼ cup sea salt

Serves 4–6

Put 250 ml/ 1 cup water and the sugar in a pan over medium heat. Bring to the boil. Set aside.

Combine the lime juice, zest of 1 lime, triple sec, beer and tequila. Pour into a lipped baking sheet. Add the sugar syrup. Freeze for 1 hour, then scrape the contents with a fork once an hour until frozen into crystals.

For the lime sugar rim, combine the remaining lime zest with the sugar and salt. Dip the rims of 4–6 small glasses in water, then in the lime sugar. Serve the granita in the sugared glasses.

SARDINES WITH CAMPARI, PEACH & FENNEL

2 mackerel fillets or
  6 sardines
2 ripe peaches, pitted
2 tablespoons Campari
3 tablespoons olive oil
1 teaspoon sea salt
1 tablespoon
  peppercorn-sized
  breadcrumbs
1 handful rustic
  croutons, made by
  toasting a piece of

sourdough and ripping
  it into small pieces
1 fennel bulb, cut into
  thin strips, fennel tops
  reserved
1 handful mint leaves
1 teaspoon black pepper
1 handful black olives,
  pitted

Serves 2

VENICE

This supper is inspired by the two great drinks of Venice: the Bellini and the Spritz. A Spritz in Italy is a dangerous thing. It may look like a drink for ladies toting parasols, but there's a reason why truck drivers also partake of one at the end of a long day. They pack a mean punch, melding the grunt of Campari or Aperol with wine and a splash of sparkling water.

This dish uses the bitterness of Campari as a foil for the sweetness of peaches and the saltiness of small fish common to Venetian restaurants. It also borrows one of the techniques of a Bellini. At Harry's Bar, a classic Bellini is made by grating the peach, rather than pulverizing it in a blender. This gives a pliable purée which does double duty here in a marinade and dressing. This wings me straight to Venice, and the colours on the plate echo the sight of a sunset over San Marco. Except here you'll find far fewer tourists clogging your view.

If using sardines, butterfly them: remove the heads, trim the fins and slit the fish open from the belly down to the tail. Open the fish like a book and place, skin-side up, on a board. Press down with your hand along the backbone to flatten it. Turn the fish over and pull out the backbone, cutting off the tail. Finally, pick out any obvious bones left behind.

Finely grate one of the peaches into a bowl and add the Campari. Set half of this mixture aside in another bowl. Marinate the fish in half of the mixture for 20 minutes.

Heat a frying pan (or barbecue) over high heat. Add 1 tablespoon of the olive oil, the salt and a layer of breadcrumbs. This will help prevent the flesh of the fish sticking. Cook the fish for 4 minutes on one side, until the flesh is opaque. Flip and cook for 2 minutes on the other side. Add the croutons to the pan to toast them further.

Slice the remaining peach into slivers. Mix them with the fennel, croutons, mint leaves and pepper. Whisk the reserved peach-Campari mixture with the remaining olive oil and sprinkle over the fennel salad. Toss to coat. Serve the fish fillets on top of the salad. Garnish with fennel tops and black olives.

TOMATO KEFTEDES WITH TZATZIKI

Tomato keftedes

400 g/14 oz. ripe cherry tomatoes
½ red onion, very finely chopped
5 g/¼ cup basil, chopped
10 g/½ cup mint, chopped
1 teaspoon dried oregano
5 g/¼ cup flat leaf parsley, chopped
100 g/¾ cup self-raising flour
250 ml/1 cup olive oil
750 ml/3 cups sunflower or canola oil

Tzatziki

1 cucumber
350 g/12 oz. Greek yogurt
2 tablespoons lemon juice
2 garlic cloves, finely chopped or grated
1 tablespoon extra virgin olive oil
salt and black pepper

heavy-based pan

Makes 16 keftedes, enough for 4 as part of a mezze

Tomato keftedes

Put the tomatoes in a large bowl and pinch them so that the juices spurt out (be careful to pinch them facing downwards, otherwise you'll end up with pulp in your eye). Keep pinching and tearing at the flesh until you're left with a pile of seeds, juices and pulp.

Add the onion, basil, mint, oregano, parsley and salt and pepper to the pulp. You can use a potato masher at this point to make sure everything is well incorporated.

Add half the flour and stir. Add the second half slowly. You want a thick and sticky paste the texture of a thick batter.

Heat the oils in a deep, heavy-based pan until small bubbles form on the surface. Make sure the oil is at least 5 cm/2 inches deep. Use a greased tablespoon to drop in the batter. After 30 seconds, rotate the fritter so it doesn't stick to the bottom. Fry for another 30 seconds or until the outside is crispy and deep red. Drain well on kitchen paper. Fry no more than 3 at a time.

Season the fritters with salt and serve hot with tzatziki.

SANTORINI

Ammoudi is a fishing village 214 steps below the town of Oia in Santorini. You can take the stairs, drive down the twirlingly steep road or hitch a ride on the back of a donkey. At the bottom you'll find a smattering of tavernas nudging against water so clear you'd swear it was glass. Down here the blazing summer sun seems less harsh. There's a breeze that whispers across the water, making small boats nod enthusiastically. Around the corner and across the rocks is one of the best swimming spots on the island.

But the real reason you'll want to descend to Ammoudi is for tomato fritters. The black volcanic soil the tomatoes grow in produces candy-sweet, ruby gems. Luckily there are plenty of flavours and textures at play, so even if your tomatoes are bog standard you can still recreate some of the magic at home. They are simply onions and a knot of green herbs bound together with pinched tomato flesh and flour, then fried until they're as dark red as a British backpacker's neck. Serve with tzatziki, fava and meatballs for a true taste of Santorini.

Tzatziki

Cut the cucumber in half lengthways and use a teaspoon to scrape out the seeds. Grate the 2 halves into a clean tea towel. Gather up the edges and squeeze out as much excess liquid as you can. Whisk together the yogurt, lemon juice, garlic and olive oil. Add the squeezed cucumber flesh and stir.

This is lovely as part of a mezze with Fava with Lamb Meatballs (page 50).

ATHENS

'Eat the rich', reads some of the fresh graffiti on the ancient white walls. On our first night in Athens we sat with the Temple of Hephaestus below and the pristine Acropolis above picking at meatballs and fava. The slurry of yellow split peas scented with garlic and bay was soothing, in strong contrast with the aggression that simmered among the frustrated citizens around us. Over dinner we made a list of the things we are in debt to the Greeks for. Chief among them we counted democracy; the plays of Sophocles and sturdy pastes like these. Fava is an unsung hero of the mezze platter. It pairs with lamb meatballs and grilled/broiled meat better than anything I've encountered. It's comforting and delicious both cold and warm. And, perhaps best of all in lean times, it's very, very cheap.

FAVA WITH LAMB MEATBALLS

Fava
- 180 g/1 cup dried yellow split peas, rinsed
- 1 bay leaf
- 1 teaspoon salt
- 2 tablespoons dry white wine
- 3 garlic cloves, crushed
- 60 ml/¼ cup extra virgin olive oil
- 2 teaspoons dried oregano
- 2 tablespoons good red wine vinegar
- 2 tomatoes, finely diced
- 1 tablespoon capers, fried for 30 seconds in 1 tablespoon olive oil
- black pepper

Lamb meatballs
- 600 g/1¼ lbs. minced/ground lamb
- 1 teaspoon ground cinnamon
- 3 garlic cloves, crushed
- 50 g/1 cup fresh breadcrumbs
- 2 tablespoons oregano, chopped
- 1 egg, lightly beaten
- 1 teaspoon cracked black pepper
- salt

Makes 32 golf-ball-sized meatballs; serves 4 with pita bread and a tomato salad

Fava

Put the split peas in a large pan and cover with cold water by 5 cm/2 inches. Bring to the boil. Reduce the heat to medium and skim off any scum that appears. Add the bay leaf and simmer for 40 minutes. Add the salt and simmer for 20 more minutes until the split peas are soft. Drain off any excess liquid and remove the bay leaf.

Add the white wine, garlic and olive oil and blend with a stick blender until smooth. Allow to cool. Season with dried oregano, red wine vinegar, salt and black pepper. Top with finely diced tomatoes, fried capers and a drizzle of olive oil and serve alongside the meatballs.

Meatballs

Preheat the oven to 200°C (400°F) Gas 6. Line a baking sheet with baking parchment.

In a large bowl, combine the lamb with the rest of the ingredients and season with salt and pepper. Mix well with your hands. Create golf ball-shaped meatballs with a tablespoon of mixture and flatten slightly. Place on the prepared baking sheet and bake for 15–20 minutes or until cooked through.

THE SOUTH OF FRANCE
(TO WALLOW IN PINK WINE)

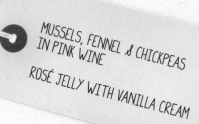

MUSSELS, FENNEL & CHICKPEAS IN PINK WINE

ROSÉ JELLY WITH VANILLA CREAM

There are places on earth where it is unnatural to feel poorly, and Menton is one of them. Menton sits on the cusp of Italy and France, keeping watch over the Mediterranean. The public gardens brim with roses, the boulevards are wide and the harbour houses white boats that easily sleep 14. While the soundtrack of neighbouring Monaco is of Ferraris, small dogs and helicopters, Menton has a hum of subdued satisfaction. This is a place designed for gold-rimmed sunglasses and nautical stripes. When strolling the promenades, you should have braiding around your cuff – not handkerchiefs tucked inside them.

The honking travel flu we brought in with us mocked the quiet elegance of the city. What saved the trip were the rose-coloured glasses, care of the copious amounts of salmon-hued wine we sipped (for medicinal purposes, of course).

By the time we made it to Marseille, we were ourselves again. Fish soup, more pink wine and dips in the Mediterranean proved perfect salves.

This menu is both a celebration of the south of France and the perfect thing to consume if you're a little under the weather. The mussels are a medley of everything I love about Marseille, without the tedious politics of what's invited into a bouillabaisse. There's some pleasing sweetness from softened fennel and shellfish. Then there's the novelty of chickpeas playing hide-and-seek in the shells. These nutty pulses contribute not only ballast, but echo the flavours of the city's famed chickpea flour crêpes (*socca*).

When it comes to dessert, there are two things that make my spirits bloom. One is fresh flowers. The other, I've since learnt, is a glass of pink wine. If The Hungry One is flailing, the only thing he'll willingly partake in is jelly. This rosé/rose jelly has become the cure-all.

If you're preparing this menu, you'll have to open at least one bottle of pink wine so you can steam the mussels and complete the jelly. There will be a splash left for the cook. Take my advice: open another; pretend you can see boats nudging the horizon; clear your sinuses and take some time to smell the roses. No matter how you were feeling when you started, healthy contentedness comes from this.

MUSSELS, FENNEL & CHICKPEAS IN PINK WINE

1 kg/2¼ lbs. mussels
1 tablespoon olive oil
3 garlic cloves, thinly sliced
1 fennel bulb, trimmed and
    finely diced
1 x 400-g/14-oz. can chickpeas,
    rinsed and drained
200 ml/¾ cup dry rosé wine
4 tablespoons chopped flat
    leaf parsley
bread, for dipping
1 recipe Aïoli (page 57)

large, heavy, lidded saucepan

Serves 2

Put the mussels in a sink of cold water. Get rid of any that are open and won't close when you tap them against the side of the sink. Remove the hairy tuft of beard from each mussel.

Heat the olive oil in a heavy-based saucepan. Sauté the garlic and fennel over medium heat until translucent. Add the chickpeas and toss to coat them in the olive oil. Add the mussels, wine and half the parsley to the pan. Turn up the heat and clamp on the lid. Steam for 5 minutes until all the mussels have opened (discard any that don't).

Transfer the mussels, chickpeas and broth to 2 bowls. Top with the remaining parsley. Place the bread and aïoli in the centre of the table, along with an extra bowl for the shells.

ROSÉ JELLY WITH VANILLA CREAM

450 ml/1¾ cups rosé wine
petals from 1 unsprayed
　white or pink rose
3 tablespoons sugar
3 gelatine leaves
1 tablespoon rose water
1 egg white, beaten
1 tablespoon icing/
　confectioners' sugar
½ teaspoon vanilla paste
2 tablespoons softly
　whipped cream

2 wine glasses

Serves 2

Pour the wine into a pan with the rose petals. Bring to the boil. Take it off the heat when the first bubbles rise up. Add the sugar, clamp on a lid and allow to steep for 10 minutes.

Put the gelatine leaves in a bowl with cold water and leave to soften for 5 minutes. Fish the rose petals out of the wine and set aside.

Squeeze the excess water from the gelatine leaves (they will feel flaccid and slimy). Stir them into the hot wine until they have dissolved.

Add the rose water to the hot liquid and gelatine. Pour the mixture into 2 wine glasses and allow to set in the fridge for 6 hours.

Preheat the oven to 50°C (125°F), or the lowest setting. Dry the reserved rose petals gently with kitchen paper, then dip in egg white and dust with icing/confectioners' sugar. Transfer to a wire rack and place in the oven for 1 hour, until dry.

Stir the vanilla paste into the whipped cream. Serve the jelly with the cream and the crystallized rose petals over the top.

HORSERADISH VODKA & LANGOUSTINES

300 ml/1¼ cups vodka
50 g/2 oz. fresh
    horseradish, cut into
    matchsticks
½ lemon
3–4 langoustines per
    person
brown bread, to serve

Aïoli
2 egg yolks
120 ml/½ cup mild olive
    oil, or half olive oil and
    half vegetable oil
2 garlic cloves, crushed
½ lemon
salt and black pepper

Serves 4–6 as a starter/
appetizer

The day before serving, combine the vodka and horseradish in the vodka bottle and screw the lid on. Let it sit at room temperature for 12 hours, then place in the freezer to chill.

Bring a big pan of water to the boil. Add a generous pinch of salt and the lemon. Set up another bowl with iced water. Boil 4–6 langoustines at a time for 90 seconds, then plunge them into the iced water. Serve the cooled langoustines with the aïoli and chilled shots of horseradish vodka on the side.

Aïoli
Whisk the egg yolks in a clean bowl for 30 seconds. Slowly trickle in the oil and continue whisking until you have a thick and glossy mayonnaise. Stir in the garlic, grated zest of the lemon and a good squeeze of the juice. Season with salt and pepper.

If the mayonnaise splits, don't throw it out, just get a clean bowl and whisk another egg yolk. Slowly trickle in the split mixture.

STOCKHOLM

If you like open sandwiches, it's easy to eat well in Stockholm. If, like The Hungry One, you feel robbed and baffled by something you consider half made, then life will be harder. That is, until you find the langoustines. Unlike other crustaceans, langoustines don't change colour when they are cooked. These salmon-pink, skinny lobsters remind me of 20-year-old Australian kids at the beach, sunburned and scrawny from time spent cavorting in clear waters.

A langoustine's flesh is both rich and sweet. What it cries for is something clean. The warming clarity of horseradish vodka fills that brief. A small, iced shot glass served alongside is the perfect start and finish to a meal that is the definition of elegant sufficiency.

As for how to get at the meat inside the langoustine; first pinch the sides of the belly in on themselves, like you're squeezing ribs into a corset. The casing should crack down the centre. Then peel the shell and the tail off and pluck out the meat. It's no harder than navigating a topless sandwich.

MINIBAR COCKTAIL PARTY

This is for the times when you desperately need a cocktail but can't quite bring yourself to change out of the fluffy robe.

Somewhere in the hotel room there's a wee fridge chocked with bottles of booze in sizes best suited for dolls. You'll find soft drinks and juices crouching in there too. On the bench above there's a kettle, tea bags, instant coffee and sugar. And if you pick up the phone you can probably get ice and some wedges of lemon sent up to your room.

You could open the half-bottle of Chardonnay and pour yourself a glass. You could have a nip of whiskey. Or you could get a little creative and fix yourself one of these.

Citrus gin fizz

This is a salve for humid nights spent wandering around foreign cities. This is what you turn to while waiting for the air conditioning to click over to Arctic.

Take a tall water glass and add four cubes of ice, one small bottle of gin, the juice of half a lemon and half a sachet of white sugar. Firmly affix a saucer to the top and shake vigorously. Use the saucer to strain into a tumbler. Top with soda water.

Coffee martini

For when you need to be pepped up – jet lag be damned.

Make a cup of instant coffee. Drink half of it. Leave the other half to cool while you have a shower. Mix the remaining coffee with a sachet of sugar and a small bottle of vodka. Shake over ice using a tall glass and saucer. Strain. Drink while you eat a Toblerone and summon the energy to leave your room.

Peppermint tea martini

This is one to calm you down – possibly after one too many coffee martinis.

Make a cup of peppermint tea. Drink three-quarters of it and leave the rest to chill. Add a sachet of sugar and the small bottle of vodka. Muddle with ice and strain. Sip while you click over hundreds of channels and dip in and out of a black and white movie in a language you don't quite understand.

Emergency martini

Maybe your partner's plane was delayed, your wallet stolen or you're staring down visa issues. This drink is the short answer to any bad day.

Take the small bottle of gin (two if they have them). Shake over ice. Add an olive or two. Drink. If you're feeling particularly dirty, swish in some of the olive brine.

Cuba Libre

For those nights when all you want to do is run away to Cuba. They usually appear when you're trapped for ten hours sitting in a hotel conference room, with a group of others who also wish they were anywhere else.

Take the bottle of Coke. Take the bottle of rum. Try your luck on a lime from reception, or one of the table arrangements in the lobby. Mix over ice and drink.

Shandy

If the generic beer in the minibar is a shattering disappointment, you have two options. The first involves chilling the beverage so hard that the result is more of an exercise in temperature than taste. The second is a shandy. Confidently add a slash of lemonade to the beverage and drink; potentially while making Jenga towers out of pretzels and peanuts and lamenting your lost youth.

Hot buttered rum

Perfect for when it's very cold or dark outside and you're in need of a hot toddy or comfort. Note: this one requires you to get a little loose with pats of butter from the breakfast buffet.

Combine in a mug one sachet of raw sugar, one small bottle of dark rum and one pat of butter. Top with boiling water. Stir. Drink. Sleep.

White wine spritzer

Perfect for when you need a drink and don't want to imbibe too much booze too soon. It's what you turn to when you've got a conference call with the Sydney office still to take at 1.15am. It's also just right when the white wine in the minibar is an insipid Pinot

Grigio. Combine the sparkling water and white wine and consume while researching somewhere better to go out tomorrow night.

Mimosa/pineapple bellini

This cocktail is best drunk in the morning, after a funeral or on Christmas day.

Crack open the small bottle of Champagne. It will probably be both expensive and a disappointment. Distract yourself from both of those facts by stretching it a little further with a dash of orange or pineapple juice.

Lazy sangria

If you want to get a party started in a small space, this is what you need.

Mix a small bottle of red wine, half a small bottle of orange juice and half a can of lemonade with whatever fruit you can scavenge from the complimentary fruit bowl (except bananas – they're just going to go limpid and grey). Add some brandy or Cointreau if you fancy giving it an extra kick. Potentially rinse out the vase from the coffee table to use as a vessel. Enjoy.

ESTORIL

It's only 35 minutes on the train from Lisbon to Estoril. Every 20 minutes the trains snake past the beaches of the Cascais. Estoril is near the end of the line. At one end of the beach is a castle owned by the royal family of Monaco. At the other end of the promenade is a restaurant. The menus are laminated and there's a note on the bathroom door reminding you that clothes and shoes are required before entering.

We've come to the Portuguese coast to celebrate. All the birthday boy wanted was a swim in some surf and some seafood. We share a pitcher of sangria the size of a sandcastle and a shallow puddle of garlic prawns. All that is missing from the party are our friends.

One week later we recreated the feast in London. In this version the sangria and garlic prawns hugged each other. There's a slick of red wine syrup and diced apple and mint for texture. There's still plenty of garlicky oil to dunk your bread in. It's not quite the same as melding prawns, cocktails and friends all together by the Portuguese seaside, but as far as compromises go, it's a good one.

SANGRIA PRAWNS

700 g/1½ lbs. fresh
   prawns/shrimp (or
   350 g/¾ lb. shelled
   prawns/shrimp)
1 orange
1 teaspoon sugar
   (optional)
250 ml/1 cup fruity
   red wine
160 ml/⅔ cup olive oil
zest of ½ lemon
6 garlic cloves
   (4 thinly sliced,
   2 crushed)
½ red chilli, diced
½ small green apple,
   diced
1 handful mint,
   roughly chopped
salt and black pepper
bread, to serve

Serves 4 as part of a tapas-style meal, with bread and salad, or generous meal for 2

Preheat the oven to 200°C (400°F) Gas 6.

Break the heads off the prawns/shrimp and peel off the shell and legs. Keep the tails on for presentation. Slit their backs with a knife and lift out the 'poo shoot' (the black vein). Put the cleaned prawns in a bowl.

Using a vegetable peeler, make 3 long strips of orange zest (half the orange's zest in total). Put the strips of zest in a saucepan and add the red wine. Heat over high heat until reduced by two-thirds and the wine is syrupy. Taste and if it's too acrid, add the sugar. Put the prawns in a baking dish. Pour over the olive oil. Grate in the remaining orange zest and the lemon zest. Add the garlic and chilli.

Cover with foil and cook in the oven for about 15–18 minutes (the larger the prawns, the longer they will take to cook). Once cooked, the prawns should be pink and firm, but not stiff to the touch. Drizzle the prawns with the red wine syrup and top with the diced apple and chopped mint. Season with salt and pepper.

Serve with bread on the side to mop up the garlic/red wine juices.

DAEJEON

Confession: I haven't been to the outskirts of Daejeon, Korea. Perhaps I should have. At 9.30pm on a warm night in Sydney a decade ago, my phone skirted across the table. On the other end was The Hungry One. He was on a bicycle, halfway through a solo trip across Asia. It was pitch black and he was very, very lost. He wanted to hear a friendly voice. Then the phone cut out. I didn't hear from him for another 10 hours. I needn't have worried. Soon he was enjoying a large bowl of *bulgogi* and drinking cheap Haite beer. With every bite of barbecued beef he said a silent thank you to the Korean grandmother who cycled 45 minutes out of her way to escort him out of the darkness, back to the bus station.

We do lots of things better as a team. Travelling is one of them. I read the maps. He handles the currency. This salad is another project that benefits from teamwork. While one person shreds the iceberg lettuce and nashi pear, the other grills the meat and the eggs. While egg is more traditionally found in the Korean *bibimbap* than in *bulgogi*, I've included it here because he likes it. And because he found his way back safely to me, I let him have it.

BULGOGI SALAD

Beef marinade
3 tablespoons soy sauce
2 tablespoons sugar
½ tablespoon sesame oil
3 garlic cloves, finely chopped
1 tablespoon toasted sesame seeds
pinch of chilli powder
1 teaspoon black pepper
5 cm/2 inches fresh ginger, grated

Salad
400 g/14 oz. rib-eye steak, thinly sliced (partially freezing the beef will help you cut clean slices)
½ onion, sliced into very thin half moons
4 eggs
1 nashi pear, cored and cut into thin slivers
¼ iceberg lettuce, finely shredded
¼ white cabbage, finely shredded

Serves 4

Whisk together the ingredients for the beef marinade. Add the steak and onion slices and massage to combine. Cover and place in the fridge for 1 hour.

Heat a barbecue or frying pan over high heat and pan-fry or grill the steak and onions in single layers until the edges are crisp. Fry the eggs, keeping the yolks runny.

Combine the nashi pear, lettuce and cabbage and divide between 4 bowls. Top with the beef, onion and fried eggs. Serve with chilli sauce.

MARRAKECH
(TO MINGLE WITH SPICES, ORANGES & DONKEYS)

PIGEON PASTILLA
AVOCADO MILKSHAKE POPSICLES

There were donkeys and dust. The further we ventured from the centre of the medina, the more we got lost. We clung on to each other's bags and used the call to prayer as our trail of breadcrumbs to find the way back. Along the way we got waylaid, browsing for carpets and cushions we couldn't carry and shoes that didn't quite fit.

While the streets of Marrakech reminded me of the bustle of Bangkok, inside our riad it was cool and quiet. For breakfast we ate crêpes; a legacy from the French. In the heat of the day we had berber bread with the texture of petrified kitchen sponges and thin links of spicy merguez sausage.

We found a sweetness that wove its way through Djemaa El Fna Square. Grinning monkeys tried hard to grab onto our hands. Avocados were being blended with condensed milk and poured into plastic bags for shakes the colour of pistachio gelato. At the end of every cup of mint tea, when weathered men would entice us to buy a carpet, was a lump of sugar. And we were convinced that the orange juice for sale on the square must have been jazzed up with something. It tasted like shots of pure sunshine.

Even the savoury dishes we ate, as on the shaded balconies near the souk, were sweet. Prunes and apricots relaxed into bubbling tagines and sugar was present in the pastillas. My favourite of these light pies was made of pigeon. Shreds of dark poultry meat wrapped up with the squish of ground almonds, mysterious notes of spice and squiggles of cooked egg. Traditionally, it's made with a wafer-thin type of pastry called *warka* – at home I substitute the light crackle of filo/phyllo. At the very end they're dusted so they more closely resemble confection. At the time we wondered if it was all too sweet, too much.

The days we spent pottering around the medina of Marrakech were just four before a bomb went off at the Argana Café, killing 17 people, including one British travel writer.

Sometimes when remembering a holiday, it can be best to focus on the sweet and the light. This is a menu which allows you to do just that. Invite friends around. Eat poultry pies with blistered oranges on cushions on your floor. Light candles. Enjoy pale green popsicles. Sip mint tea. Add a little more sugar to the bottom of your cup if you think it calls for it. Then reach out and touch the palm of someone you adore.

PIGEON PASTILLA

A pastilla is made up of four parts.

There's the shredded pigeon flesh. There's an egg-like curd, made by reducing the poaching stock, which is mixed and cooked with the beaten eggs. Then there's the almond mixture, which is a combination of butter, almonds, cinnamon and a touch of sugar. Then there's the pastry crust. This is the kind of dish that's good to make over the course of a Saturday afternoon.

3 x 150-g/5 oz. pigeons
   (or substitute other
   game birds, duck or
   chicken legs and
   thighs)
2 tablespoons ras el
   hanout (a Moroccan
   spice blend – you can
   substitute a fragrant
   combination of ground
   coriander, cumin,
   turmeric, cardamom,
   nutmeg and cloves)
1 pinch saffron, or
   1 teaspoon powdered
   saffron
100 g/6½ tablespoons
   butter
1 onion, finely diced
1 tablespoon olive oil
1 cinnamon stick
a piece of fresh ginger
   the size of a wine cork

1 teaspoon salt
4 eggs, beaten
2 tablespoons icing/
   confectioners' sugar
2 tablespoons ground
   cinnamon
100 g/3½ oz. ground
   almonds
12–15 sheets filo/phyllo
   pastry
4 teaspoons orange-
   flower water (or rose
   water)
2 tablespoons flaked/
   slivered almonds

To serve
2 oranges

Makes 4 individual
pastillas

Pigeons

Clean and pat the pigeons dry with kitchen paper. In a heavy-based casserole dish, toast the ras el hanout, powdered saffron (if using) and cinnamon stick. When the spices are nutty and fragrant, take them out of the pan and set aside to cool. Roll the pigeons in the toasted spice mixture.

Melt 30 g/2 tablespoons of the butter in the pan until it's gently foaming and add the onion Cook slowly until translucent.

Add 1 tablespoon olive oil to the pan. Turn up the heat and add the pigeons. Sear the outside of the birds, turning regularly with tongs. Add the cinnamon, 360 ml/1½ cups warm water and the ginger. If using saffron stems, now is the time to add them. Turn down the heat to medium. Clamp the lid on the casserole dish and let the birds simmer for 1 hour. Turn off the heat and let them cool in the stock.

When the pigeons are cool enough to handle, pull the meat off the bones and put it in a bowl to one side. Season the meat with salt.

Egg curd

Return the poaching liquid to a high heat and boil until reduced by half. Remove the cinnamon stick and piece of ginger.

Pour in the beaten eggs and cook gently, stirring frequently, until it looks like seized scrambled eggs. Cook as much of the liquid out of it as you can. Turn off the heat and strain the mixture to remove any extra liquid.

Almond filling

Melt 50 g/3½ tablespoons butter and stir it into the ground almonds with 1 tablespoon of the ground cinnamon and 1 tablespoon of the icing/confectioners' sugar.

Assemble the pastilla

Preheat the oven to 180°C (350°F) Gas 4.

Melt the remaining butter. Lay out the filo/phyllo pastry and cover it with a damp tea towel. Take

2 sheets and dab each one with melted butter. Place them on top of each other and cut them into a circle 30 cm/12 inches in diameter. Reserve the trimmings under the damp tea towel.

Add 2½ tablespoons of the almond mixture to the centre of the circle. Drizzle the mixture with a few drops of the orange-flower water. Top that with 2½ tablespoons of the egg mixture. Place a quarter of the shredded pigeon meat on top.

Use the pastry trimmings to layer over the top of the mound, cupping your hands to tuck it down, as though you were smoothing the base of a sandcastle.

Fold one side of the pastry circle up towards the centre. You want to create a hexagon. So, 60 degrees to the left, fold another side up. Then again at another 60 degrees. Then again, and again and again. You should have a hexagon-shaped parcel and the pastry should meet in the middle

Brush with melted butter to seal. Gently flip the pastilla over. Brush the top with melted butter and sprinkle one-quarter of the flaked/slivered almonds over the top.

Repeat the process to make the 3 more pastillas.

To bake the pastillas, put them on a baking sheet lined with greaseproof paper and bake in the preheated oven for 35 minutes. You want the pastry to be brown and crispy.

Dust with the remaining cinnamon and icing sugar. Serve with a green salad dressed with the juice of half an orange and olive oil. Alternatively, serve with caramelized orange: cut the oranges in half and cook, cut-side down, in the pan you melted the butter in, until brown and caramelized. This provides a bit of a sauce and a nice citrus kick.

AVOCADO MILKSHAKE POPSICLES

4 medium-sized ripe avocados
1 tablespoon grated orange zest
250 ml/1 cup sweetened condensed milk

4 plastic cups
4 spoons or popsicle sticks

Serves 4

Use a spoon to remove the flesh from the avocados, discarding the skin and pit/stone. Cut off any brown bits.

Put the avocado, orange zest and condensed milk in a blender and process until smooth.

Pour into plastic cups and place in the freezer for 1 hour.

Insert the popsicle sticks in the centre of the half-frozen popsicles and freeze for another 4 hours.

To remove from the plastic cups, dip in hot water for 5 seconds.

Winter

FEASTS BEST EATEN
WHEN HUNKERING
DOWN IN FRONT OF
A FIRE

POST CARD

WHITSTABLE

Oysters are at their gleaming best in winter. To me, they should always be served cold, with a cheek of lemon at 10 o'clock and a glass of white wine at 2. That's unless they're poached. The first time I tried poached oysters was at The Sportsman – a stellar restaurant and pub at Whitstable, near the mouth of the Thames. Those fat and happy bivalves were gilded with cream, poached in their shells and topped with salty roe and pickled cucumbers. They were a swaddle of comfort coupled with the sea. This version takes the lead from there. My white wine and lemon are still present, though now they sit inside the shell. It's brightened with flaked almonds and fronds of fennel flutter over the top like seaweed on the shore. Serve three oysters each with good-quality bread and yellow butter for an elegant starter, or one each as a canapé.

POACHED OYSTERS

6 oysters, shucked
1 tablespoon crème fraîche or double/ heavy cream
1 tablespoon dry white wine
1 tablespoon grated lemon zest
2 tablespoons shaved fennel
1 teaspoon fennel tops

1 tablespoon flaked/ slivered almonds, toasted
black pepper
sourdough bread and butter, to serve

steamer with a lid

Serves 2 as a starter/ appetizer with drinks

Pour off some of the oyster's natural juices. Layer the shells so that they stay upright in a steamer basket.

Carefully dot the oysters with crème fraiche or cream and drizzle with white wine and lemon zest.

Bring the water under the oysters to a medium simmer and put the lid on the steamer. Steam the oysters for 5–7 minutes.

Top with wafts of shaved fennel, fennel fronds, toasted almonds and black pepper.

Serve with good sourdough bread and butter.

THE HUNTER VALLEY

The vineyards of the Hunter Valley are where we got married. Two and a half hours from Sydney, it's an area best known for ballsy Shirazes (with their classic notes of 'sweaty saddle'), pleasant vistas and mildly twee stores stocked with olive oil and nut-studded chocolate. A day of driving around the vineyards traditionally ended with us sharing a bottle of red at the Tuscany Wine Estate and drinking in their view over the valley. This spot has the added lure of being next door to the Binnorie Dairy and their famed *labna*, a strained yogurt cheese. These tartines transport us straight back to the weekends we spent in the Hunter Valley planning our wedding. On top of the charred bread and labna are blistered red grapes and toasted nuts. As for the labna, you could buy it from the Binnorie Dairy. Or you could make it yourself with the aid of a few hours, some yogurt and cloth. This is best eaten while letting a glass of good red breathe, avoiding finalizing seating charts and musing about whether doing your first dance to Van Morrison's *Brown-Eyed Girl* is too much of a cliché.

TARTINES WITH LABNA, ROASTED RED GRAPES & WALNUTS

Labna
250 g/1 cup full-fat Greek yogurt
1 teaspoon salt

Tartines
60 red grapes (a medium bunch)
100 g/¾ cup (about 40) walnuts, roughly chopped
2 tablespoons olive oil
1 teaspoon sugar
4 slices of good sourdough bread
½ garlic clove
salt and black pepper

Serves 4 for lunch, as part of a tasting plate-style meal

Begin the labna at least 6 hours before you plan on eating. Mix together the Greek yogurt and the salt. Line a strainer with 2 pieces of muslin/cheesecloth, or J-cloth/Chux. Set the strainer and the cloth over a bowl. Pour the yogurt and the salt into the strainer, cover the top with the ends of the cloth and allow to strain for at least 6 hours.

After 6 hours, squeeze the cloth to help the curds separate from the whey. The yogurt should have the consistency of cream cheese. You should end up with 125 g/½ cup labna. Transfer to a covered container and chill in the fridge until ready to use.

Alternatively, you can roll it into small balls and cover them with olive oil (it will last in the fridge for about 1 week).

Preheat the oven to 220°C (425°F) Gas 7. Put the grapes and walnuts on a baking sheet. Sprinkle with olive oil and sugar. Roast for 20 minutes, until the grapes have started to wrinkle. Grill/broil or toast the sourdough. When it is nicely brown, rub the toast with the cut side of the garlic.

Spread the slices of toast with a tablespoon of labna, then pile on the grapes and walnuts. Season generously with salt and pepper.

BLUE MOUNTAINS

An hour west of Sydney loom the Blue Mountains. They're home to the Three Sisters rock formation and some of Australia's best apples. Beyond them is the bush hamlet where I first attempted camping. There's a frontier-braving pluckiness that happy campers share. Here are my thoughts – most days we work hard to earn a crust so we can have lights that go on and off. Why flee that to sleep on hard surfaces? It seems it's about being close to nature, collecting stories and learning a few things about yourself. Here are some things I gleaned from my first effort:

* Men like making fires.
* Without access to water, baby wipes are your friend.
* Food that doesn't require plates is worth its weight in gold.
* Marshmallows are good for morale. So is red wine.
* It's wise to stop drinking a good hour or two before you go to sleep.
* Practise the squatting thing at least once before you turn in. It'll save you from praying you haven't soiled your socks in the pitch dark.

This pumpkin soup is in memory of the glow of campfires and the sweet taste of Blue Mountain Bilpin apples. There's even the grit of pebbles, recreated in a sweet nut crumble. You could take it in a Thermos next time you brave the elements. Or eat it in the warmth of your home. I think you can guess which path I choose.

ROAST APPLE & PUMPKIN SOUP WITH MAPLE NUT CRUMBLE

4 Pink Lady apples, peeled, cored and roughly chopped into eighths
1.4 kg/3 lbs. pumpkin, skinned and chopped into pieces the same size as the apple
2 onions, quartered
a piece of fresh ginger the size of a wine cork, peeled and sliced
6 garlic cloves, skin on
4 tablespoons olive oil
1.5 litres/6 cups warm chicken or vegetable stock
2 tablespoons double/heavy cream and maple syrup
salt and black pepper

Serves 4

Preheat the oven to 200°C (400°F) Gas 6.

Put the apple, pumpkin, onion, ginger and garlic in a roasting pan. Drizzle with olive oil and season with salt and pepper. Roast for 45 minutes, until golden. (Roast for another 30 minutes if you have time. This will give more colour and sweetness.)

Remove from the oven. Squeeze the garlic from its skins and transfer the flesh to a saucepan. Add the pumpkin, apple, ginger and onion and any juices from the roasting pan. Pour over the warm stock and stir to combine. Process with a stick blender until very smooth. Season with salt and pepper. Heat through before serving in bowls, topped with the nut crumble, cream and maple syrup.

MAPLE NUT CRUMBLE

120 g/¾ cup mixed
   pumpkin seeds,
   hazelnuts, almonds,
   macadamia nuts
1 teaspoon salt
80 g/scant ½ cup (caster)
   sugar

Serves 4

Dry-toast the nuts and seeds in a frying pan.
Pour them onto a baking sheet lined with
baking parchment and sprinkle with salt.

Put the sugar in a pan and place over
medium heat. Swirl the pan, rather than
stirring, to mix the sugar as it melts. Cook
until all the sugar has melted and has turned
a light gold colour. Pour the molten sugar
over the top of the nuts. Be careful: the sugar
will be very, very hot. Transfer the baking
sheet to the freezer and chill for 30 minutes.
Chop the praline on the baking parchment
into rough pebbles.

A FORMULA FOR CARPET PICNICS

It lives in the imagination of every hungry, misty-eyed traveller: the vision of foraging for delicious odds and ends at local markets, then nestling down to a picnic while watching boats bob down foreign rivers, or kites skip across different skies.

Yet it doesn't always work out. Sometimes the weather won't play nicely. Other times you'll be shuffled off the grass before you've even pulled up a perch. Occasionally, the failure will be all of your own making. You'll be overwhelmed by choice during the shopping and sit down to a chaotic collection of things trapped in paper and plastic. You'll unveil three dips, five wilting wedges of cheese and a melon nobody can cut into. There won't be enough bread. And there will be an embarrassing quantity of nuts – nobody will ever let you buy just a handful.

But there's no need to give up hope when the elements are against you. There's always the option of a carpet picnic back in your hotel. As for the rest, all you need is a plan.

When facing the bounty of the great food markets of the world (all of Paris, Les Halles in Lyon, Östermalms Saluhall in Stockholm, the fish markets of Sydney, La Boqueria in Barcelona and Borough Market in London), simplicity can be the best path. I have very fond memories of picking up a rotisserie chicken from Paris' Mouffetard, a large, soft lettuce, a bunch of fresh tarragon and another of green grapes. We found a clear spot and fashioned chicken and herb lettuce

wraps. Some of the grapes went in with the wraps for a sweet pop. The rest we ate lazily while lying on the grass.

Pick one path and then follow it to the end. If all around you are cured meats to swoon for, commit to them. Buy six types to compare and contrast. Mix and match them with bread, olives and one hard cheese. Or just peel the pink strips off their paper backing, and marvel as the sweet fats gloss across your fingertips. The trick is to not run everywhere, chasing everything. Your eyes will be bigger than your stomach. And the leftovers won't fare that well in your backpack all day.

So here's a winning formula for coherent picnic feasts for small groups while travelling. Whether you consume it overlooking the Seine or draped across the floor of your hotel room: that is entirely up to you.

Formula = carbohydrate + protein + cheese + fruit

For example:

Focaccia + prosciutto + buffalo mozzarella + peaches

Layer the prosciutto over the peaches for antipasti. Make up mini sandwiches with the focaccia, ham and cheese. Then eat the leftover peaches for dessert.

Piadina + salami + goats' cheese + cherry tomatoes

Lay it all out in a spread. They're all friends. It works in any way.

Baguette + cold prawns/shrimp + ripe avocados + pears

The avocado stands in for cheese here. Muddle it into a dip for the prawns/shrimp, or slices with pears on baguette for sweet crostini. It's the gentle textures that unite these elements as much as the flavours.

Iceberg lettuce + rotisserie chicken + mild, soft cheese + green grapes

No proper carbs here. Instead use the lettuce as a wrap to swaddle pieces of chicken and grapes. Then swipe the remaining grapes through the drooping cheese for pudding.

White bread + jamón + manchego + apricots

The saltiness of the jamón and manchego will play well against the sweetness of both the apricots and the white bread.

Rye or bagels + smoked salmon + curds or cream cheese + apples

Here the apple provides much-needed crunch and lightness to contrast with the salmon. This is a classic, whether you're in Copenhagen or Central Park.

Pita bread + falafel + hummus + dried fruits

A quick way to make up your own pita rolls. The dried fruits make a sweet inclusion in the sandwiches. They're also excellent for picking at while finishing off the last of the beer.

Turkish bread + grilled fish + yogurt cheese + radish

There's no pudding here – just the simplicity of radishes, bread and the cleanest-tasting of cheeses. If you're still hungry, use the Turkish bread to mop up the oil the cheese came puddled in.

Rolls + speck + hard cheese + cherries

Cheese and cherries are a match made in heaven. If you need a little extra sweetness at the close, there's nothing to stop you picking up a few squares of good-quality dark chocolate for a Black Forest-inspired dessert.

LOS ANGELES

In Los Angeles it's tempting to treat celebrities like safari animals and stalk them through their native habitats.
In The Grove we thought we'd seen Jessica Simpson – but it might just have been the brief given to a plastic surgeon. We kept our eyes peeled over medium-rare burgers at In & Out, and while picking at raw protein in nose-bleedingly expensive sushi restaurants. Our closest brush with fame came as we ate toasted melts at Steven Spielberg's mother's kosher dairy restaurant, The Milky Way. Just before dessert, she pointed to the posters of Jaws, E.T. and Schindler's List, nudged us and twanged 'you do know who my son is, right?' This steak tartare reminds me of three of the most sparkling things we ate in LA: burgers, raw protein and toasted sandwiches. To me, a steak tartare carts the best bits of a burger – the grunt of meat, the lick of ketchup and the salty punch of the pickle. This mustard cheese melt is the perfect sidekick. Perhaps it's not the standard accompaniment to steak tartare. It may not be kosher, but it works.

STEAK TARTARE WITH MUSTARD CHEESE TOASTS

2 tablespoons Dijon mustard
4 anchovy fillets, finely diced
2 tablespoons ketchup
1 tablespoon Worcestershire sauce
Tabasco sauce, to taste
1 small onion, finely chopped
2 tablespoons capers, finely chopped
2 tablespoons cornichons, finely chopped
2 tablespoons flat leaf parsley, finely chopped

500 g/1 lb. 2 oz. beef sirloin, diced very finely (don't use a food processor)
4 quail egg yolks (or 2 ordinary egg yolks)
salt and black pepper
rocket/arugula, to serve

Mustard cheese toasts
2 tablespoons butter, melted
1 tablespoon hot English mustard
75 g/¾ cup grated Cheddar cheese
1 baguette, sliced into 1-cm/½-inch slices

Serves 4

Put the Dijon mustard, anchovies, ketchup and Worcestershire sauce in a large bowl and whisk. Add the onion, capers, cornichons and parsley.

Add the chopped beef to the bowl and mix well using a spoon. Season with salt and pepper and Tabasco, to taste. Divide the meat evenly among 4 chilled dinner plates.

Wash the quail egg shells well. Separate the quail eggs and nestle the yolks in half-shells on top of the tartare, for guests to mix as they like. (If you don't have quail eggs, use 2 egg yolks and whisk them with the mustard and ketchup mixture).

To make the mustard cheese toasts, combine the melted butter and English mustard and brush the mixture over the slices of baguette. Top with cheese and grill/broil for 5 minutes, until the tops are melted and bubbly. Serve with the tartare and rocket/arugula on the side.

ROAST CHICKEN WITH MUSHROOMS

1 x 1.3-kg/3-lb. chicken
1 tablespoon salt
1 tablespoon pepper
1 handful flat leaf parsley
1 onion, cut into eighths
250 g/8 oz. chestnut
   mushrooms, halved or
   quartered to the size
   of a cherry tomato
15 hazelnuts
3 garlic cloves, skin on
1 tablespoon olive oil
1½ tablespoons Dijon
   mustard
3 tablespoons double/

heavy cream or crème
   fraîche
100 g/2 cups mixed
   salad leaves (such
   as watercress, baby
   spinach, rocket/
   arugula, radicchio)
red wine vinegar and
   olive oil, to dress the
   leaves

stick blender

Serves 2, with leftover
chicken for sandwiches
or soup

Preheat the oven to 230°C (450°F) Gas 8. Dry the inside and outside of the chicken with kitchen paper.

Season the chicken with the salt and pepper. Place the parsley inside the cavity.

Put the chicken breast-side up on a roasting rack in a roasting pan – make sure that heat can circulate to most of the chicken. Put the onion, mushrooms, hazelnuts and garlic cloves around the base of the chicken. Drizzle the vegetables with olive oil.

Roast the chicken and vegetables for 45 minutes, or until the juices around the thigh run clear. When it's ready, remove the chicken from the oven, gently turn it over and let it rest, breast-side down, on the roasting rack for 15 minutes before serving (put a plate underneath to catch the juices).

Add the roasted hazelnuts to the salad leaves and dress with olive oil and red wine vinegar.

To make the mushroom sauce, squeeze the garlic cloves out of their skins into a bowl. Transfer half the cooked mushrooms, all the roasted onion segments and the chicken juices to the bowl and add the mustard and double/heavy cream. Use a stick blender to process until smooth. Stir through the remaining mushrooms and heat gently.

Carve the chicken and serve with the mushroom sauce and hazelnut and bitter leaf salad. Some French bread and good butter wouldn't go astray, either.

LAS VEGAS

One should never underestimate the power of roast chicken. This one hails from a strange place – a city with lasers that can be seen from space. Before you know it, you'll be standing misty-eyed watching a fountain dance to *Song for Guy* and streaking through a tundra of gaming machines in search of cheap tickets to a magic show. After two days in the middle of the desert, watching children spin on gaming stools while parents fed hungry poker machines, we found an oasis. One bite of Thomas Keller's signature roast chicken at Bouchon Bistro, its flesh stickily rich and skin stretched taut like an over-starched sheet, was all it took for my feelings of disquiet to soften. Chef Keller employed figs for comforting squish in the dish; my choice is mushrooms, which, with a dab of mustard and a dribbling of cream, build a sauce as soothing as a squeeze from your mum. I now know if I can feel at home in Las Vegas, I can conjure that sense anywhere. All I need is a chicken. And an oven.

BROOKLYN

A platter of ribs is not everyday food. It's a dish best eaten in familiar company, or in a part of a city where you know no one – perhaps in a borough on the other side of a big bridge. To commit to a meal of ribs you have to get your hands busy. Firstly, if they come in a rack you'll have to seek out the soft and gelatinous bits of flesh that join the bones and cut them. Then you have to pluck the meat off. There is no way to do this without getting sauce streaked down your wrists. You can do it with your fingers, transferring strings of flesh and sauce to your mouth bit by bit, but it's easier to do it with your teeth.

When ribs are good, it's about the pleasures of bone and voluptuous flesh that's smoky, sweet and has a kinky kick of heat. What they cry out for is some cut-through. To me, this rhubarb pickle is perfect. It's quirky and piquant, with some sweetness at its heart. It's a little like Brooklyn. Serve with plenty of paper towels and some stiff cocktails.

SLOW-COOKED PORK RIBS WITH RHUBARB PICKLE

1.8 kg/2 lbs. pork ribs (in a rack or as separate ribs; I find these easier to handle and you don't need to cut them before you eat them)

Marinade
300 ml/1¼ cups smoked BBQ sauce
100 ml/scant ½ cup ketchup
1 tablespoon hot English mustard
1 tablespoon grated fresh ginger
1 tablespoon grated or sliced garlic

½ tablespoon cayenne pepper (or more if you like things spicy)
2 tablespoons marmalade, melted with 1 tablespoon boiling water
150 ml/⅔ cup orange juice
3 tablespoons red wine vinegar

Rhubarb pickle
2 sticks rhubarb
2 tablespoons (caster) sugar
1½ teaspoons sea salt

Serves 2

The night before serving, make the marinade in a large sealable container. Mix all the marinade ingredients together except 100 ml/scant ½ cup of the smoked BBQ sauce and the vinegar. Then add the ribs, put the lid on and leave in the fridge overnight.

Preheat the oven to 120°C (250°F) Gas ½ and put the ribs, marinade and the vinegar in a large casserole dish. Cook for 7 hours with the lid on.

Every 2 hours or so, move the ribs around to make sure they're all covered. If the amount of fat leaching out puts you off, you can ladle off some of the cooking liquid and put it in a jar in the fridge for 2 hours to chill, then scoop off the fat that's solidified on top and return the liquid to the pan.

An hour before serving, remove the ribs from the cooking liquid, transfer to a platter and cover with foil so they don't dry out. Heat the barbecue. Before grilling, baste the ribs with the remaining BBQ sauce, thinned with a few tablespoons of the cooking liquid. Cook the ribs on the barbecue until the outside has crisped and charred a little.

Serve with rhubarb pickle and a big green salad. And wet cloths to wipe sticky hands on.

Rhubarb pickle
Wash the rhubarb stalks and trim the scraggly ends. Cut the remaining rhubarb into coins. Sprinkle the sugar and the salt over them. Shake about so that all the sides are covered.

Set aside for 1–2 hours. When the rhubarb is floppy, drain off the liquid and give them a quick rinse in a colander to remove the excess salt and sugar. Serve alongside very rich, sticky meats; roast pork belly and pork ribs are both perfect.

REYKJAVIK
(WHERE THERE ARE MUCH BETTER THINGS TO EAT THAN FERMENTED SHARK MEAT)

ICELANDIC HOT DOGS WITH REMOULADE

BLUEBERRY SKYR TRIFLE

'It tastes like evil.' That's what our taxi driver said about hakarl, the Icelandic 'delicacy' of fermented shark meat. He's not far off. My thought after eating it was that it tasted like a traumatic childhood. The small square of preserved fish had the texture of forgotten marshmallows. The smell it carried brought memories of momentarily losing control of your bladder. The taste was closest to a tuna sandwich that had lingered for a week in the bottom of a school bag.

Luckily, there are better things to give you a taste of Iceland. Roast lamb, for one (there are more sheep in Iceland than people). Or Arctic char – a fish that splashes in some of the cleanest water in the world, with flesh as pink as pinched cheeks. Then there are blueberries (*bláber*: small, indigo and very sweet and often frozen during the season that runs until August). Or spice cookies made of almonds and cinnamon with a surprising kick of black pepper. Then there's *skyr*, a light and lovely dairy product brought to Iceland from Norway by Viking settlers that's halfway between cream cheese and yogurt.

That's before we even get to the hot dogs. I did not expect to find the best hot dogs in the world in Iceland. We planned to swan around in the Blue Lagoon and trace the skies in search of northern lights. But there were no northern lights the weekend we arrived in Reykjavik, so we ate hot dogs instead.

The hot dogs are called *pylsur*. They taste properly of meat, not an indistinguishable blur of brown. The sausage snaps when you bite it. It comes with not one, but two types of onions (fried and raw). And as for condiments, in a *pylsur* there are three.

The best example of it is found at Bæjarins Beztu Pylsur. It's a name that translates as 'Town's Best'. Bæjarins Beztu has been serving these hot dogs for more than 60 years. It's an unassuming red-and-white caravan near

Reykjavik's harbour, within flinging distance of the flea market. Ordering is a simple process. You point, nod and then hand over 280 ISK. Or you can ask for *eina með öllu* (one with everything).

What you get is a long, white and fluffy bun and a smearing of goodness. The sausages are a combination of pork, beef and lamb. These days the sausages are rumoured to be braised in beer. The meat is sweet, salty and rich. Then there are the sauces: the first is a stripe of ketchup. The second is a special lightly spiced mustard the colour of tree bark. The third is remoulade, a mayonnaise that's been punched up with gherkins and capers. The taste of these made my husband's eyes light up more than the sight of *Aurora borealis* ever could. To get a true taste of Iceland at home, pair a platter of hot dogs with a dessert of Icelandic *skyr* trifle. Find some footage of *Aurora borealis* to watch on YouTube. And try very hard to forget that you ever learnt what evil tastes like.

REMOULADE

1 egg yolk
1 teaspoon Dijon mustard
180 ml/¾ cup neutral-tasting oil
1 tablespoon white wine vinegar
2 teaspoons chopped gherkin
2 teaspoons chopped capers
1 tablespoon chopped chervil

Makes 1 cup

Make the remoulade by whisking the egg yolk and mustard together. Start dripping in the oil slowly, whisking and emulsifying the oil into the egg yolk. Continue slowly dripping in the remainder of the oil, whisking all the time. When the mayonnaise is thick, add the white wine vinegar, the chopped gherkin, capers and chervil.

Depending on how heavy-handed you are with your condiments, you may have some remoulade left over. It is excellent with boiled potatoes.

BLUEBERRY SKYR TRIFLE

Cookie layer
2 egg whites
170 g/scant 1 cup sugar
1 teaspoon ground
 cinnamon
1 teaspoon cracked black
 pepper
170 g/1¾ cups ground
 almonds

Fruit and skyr
250 g/1 cup Greek yogurt
225 g/scant 1 cup low-fat
 cream cheese
200 g/1½ cups
 blueberries
juice of ½ lemon

*6 Martini glasses,
or 1 glass trifle bowl*

Serves 6

Preheat the oven to 170°C (325°F) Gas 3. Line a baking sheet with greaseproof paper.

In a large bowl, whisk the egg whites until peaks form. Add the sugar and beat until shiny. Fold in the cinnamon, black pepper and almonds. Spread the batter into a circle, 20 cm/8 inches in diameter, in the centre of the baking sheet.

Bake for 20 minutes until the outside of the disc is crisp and brown. Remove from the oven and allow to cool for 20 minutes.

Using electic beaters, mix the yogurt and the cream cheese together until smooth. Blend three-quarters of the blueberries with the lemon juice.

Crumble the cookie circle into small pieces.

Construct the trifles in martini glasses or 1 large bowl. Start with the blueberry purée, then add a layer of cookie pieces, then the 'skyr' yogurt mixture, then blueberries, then cookies, then 'skyr' and finish with blueberry purée and fresh blueberries. Refrigerate until ready to serve.

ICELANDIC HOT DOGS

6 pylsur sausages
 (or a pork and
 beef frankfurter)
350 ml/1½ cups beer
 (Viking or Gull are
 classic Icelandic beers,
 but any lager will do)
6 long white, fluffy
 hot-dog buns
6 tablespoons diced
 shallot
4 tablespoons sweet
 hot-dog mustard

(or use 3 tablespoons
 Dijon mustard mixed
 with 2 tablespoons
 brown sugar and 1
 teaspoon hot water)
4 tablespoons
 Remoulade (page 87)
4 tablespoons ketchup
6 tablespoons crispy
 deep-fried onion
 slivers

Makes 6 hot dogs

Braise the pylsur in the beer until they are hot. Split the buns down the middle and lightly toast them. Add one sausage and the diced raw shallot to each bun. Add a stripe of mustard, remoulade and ketchup down each sausage. Top with the crispy fried onions.

DUBLIN

To rediscover the taste of Ireland, some people reach for a pint of Guinness.

But Guinness is not an ale that enjoys travelling. It's something about the water at the source. It's best drunk on the seventh floor of The Guinness Storehouse with its 360-degree view over all of Dublin.

Others try a nip of Jamesons, black pudding or wandering over bridges reciting Yeats. When, like him, I find the circus animals of inspiration have deserted me, I turn to a plate of pearl barley risotto. It's a lap-rug of a dish, perfect for when the wind snaps and the sky is grey. It's a dish that's self determining. It doesn't require close supervision but if you fancy, you could check in every now and again and give it a stir while the barley unfurls and the thrifty protein from the chicken thighs poach. While parsley may not provide the 40 shades you miss from Ireland, if you add some verdant leaves halfway through cooking and then again at the end, at the very least you'll end up with two green hues on your plate.

CHICKEN & PARSLEY PEARL BARLEY RISOTTO

750 ml/3 cups chicken stock
2 tablespoons olive oil
1 onion, finely diced
3 garlic cloves, finely chopped or grated
200 g/1 cup pearl barley
100 ml/scant ½ cup white wine
400 g/14 oz. skinless chicken thighs, cut into small chunks

20 g/½ cup finely chopped flat leaf parsley
2 tablespoons double/ heavy cream or crème fraîche
zest of ½ lemon
salt and black pepper
green leaves, to serve (optional)

Serves 4

Put the stock in a large pan and bring to a simmer. Sauté the onions and the garlic in a casserole dish with the olive oil for 5 minutes until translucent. Add the pearl barley and stir it all around to mix and mingle.

Add the white wine to the pan and cook, stirring, until the wine has reduced by half. Add 2 ladles of the hot stock to the pan. Stir for 5 minutes. Add the rest of the stock to the barley and add the chicken and half the parsley. Keep it on a medium-low heat and let it gently bubble away, uncovered, for around 45 minutes, until all the stock has been absorbed into the barley. You don't need to stir constantly, just check in on it every now and again.

When the barley has puffed open and the stock has been absorbed, add the cream, remaining parsley and lemon zest. Season with salt and pepper. Serve with a pile of green leaves, if you like.

The risotto is also lovely with wilted spinach and bacon, or mushrooms and thyme.

PECORINO, PEPPER & PIG CHEEK PASTA

1 tablespoon olive oil

125 g/4 oz. guanciale, lardons or streaky bacon

1 onion, sliced into half moons

300 g/10 oz. (about 2) trimmed pig cheeks, cut into wine cork-sized chunks

1 tablespoon plain/all-purpose flour

1½ tablespoons ground black pepper, plus extra for seasoning

2 garlic cloves, sliced or finely chopped

1 teaspoon rosemary, finely chopped

360 ml/1½ cups white wine

360 ml/1½ cups water

1 leftover Parmesan cheese rind (optional)

1 potato, halved

200 g/6½ oz. linguine or bucatini

70 g/2½ oz. pecorino cheese, grated, plus extra to serve

1 teaspoon freshly grated nutmeg

salt

Serves 2

Sauté the guanciale, bacon or lardons in the olive oil until the fat flows out. Add the onion and cook for 10 minutes over medium heat until translucent.

Dust the chunks of pig cheek in flour and a few grindings of black pepper. Turn the heat up under the pan, add the cheeks and cook until browned. Add the garlic, rosemary, white wine and Parmesan rind, if you have it. When the wine comes to the boil, turn the heat down to medium and cook, uncovered, for 1 hour.

After 1 hour, top up with an additional 360 ml/1½ cups water if it is sticking on the bottom of the pan, put the lid on and cook for another 45 minutes.

Bring a pan of salted water to the boil with the potato. The starch in the potato will help boost the starch of the pasta water. Cook the pasta until al dente, remove the potato, then strain the pasta, reserving 250 ml/1 cup of the cooking water.

Remove the Parmesan rind and any pieces of fat or gristle that haven't broken down. Use 2 forks to shred the rest of the cheek meat.

Add the pecorino and black pepper to the ragu. Add the cooked pasta and just enough pasta water to bind together into a sauce. Top the pasta with fresh grated nutmeg and a little extra cheese.

ROME

Rome: the word carries visions of 'La Dolce Vita' and drifting through Piazza Navona. Then you wake up. When you need to escape toddlers being dragged through the Colosseum and furrowed brows at the Forum, Testaccio is a good place to go. For one, it's not on all the fold-out maps. It's where the old slaughterhouses were, and also where we first ate a version of this pasta. This isn't an everyday meal, but some days it will be exactly what you need. It's a tantrum of spice kicking against a mellow blanket of cheese, pork and carbohydrate. The sauce is stroppy with pepper and busy with two types of pork. It's petulant and soothing all at the same time, perfect when you need to gather yourself, regroup and find the pluck to carry on. You can make a quicker version using only lardons, but it's worth investing the time to secure a second texture of slow cooked pork cheek. Take some inspiration from the Eternal City; good things take time. Rome wasn't built in a day. This is just two hours of your afternoon.

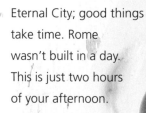

CAIRO

There are no discernible road rules in Cairo – every car, bike and cart is out for himself. The closer we got to Tahrir Square, the more we became ensnared in a mess of traffic. There were people leaning out of car windows, waving flags, yelling in jubilation. It was just one week on from the toppling of their President. We didn't intend on witnessing a revolution. When we arrived at the Great Pyramid the next morning, the area was deserted. The only sound in the burial chamber was our own breath. Later, while mixing a deep bowl of *koshary*, not far from the tanks and tangles of barbed wire, our guide tells us about the past week. He won't do business with the horsemen who give tours around the pyramids; he believes they were among the paid thugs who stormed the crowds at Tahrir. He was not there on the first day of violence; he had gone home for a rest. One of his friends had not; he died. The hardest part, he said, was staying peaceful in the face of brutality.

To cross the road in Cairo is an exercise in faith. To make it, we all step together. We calmly charge across, hoping death won't glance our way. On the other side of the chaos, we keep walking. Like the people of Cairo, we're just trying to get to the other side. And once we got there we found a sense of adrenaline and excitement that was very hard to shake.

KOSHARY

150 g/¾ cup brown lentils, rinsed well
150 g/¾ cup long-grain rice, rinsed well
2 teaspoons salt
1½ tablespoons ground cumin
180 ml/¾ cup vegetable oil
4 garlic cloves, chopped
125 ml/½ cup white wine vinegar

400 g/2 cups passata/ puréed tomato
1 teaspoon chilli powder
2 teaspoons sugar
2 large onions, sliced into thin half moons
200 g/1½ cups dried macaroni pasta
1 x 400-g/14-oz. can chickpeas, drained

Serves 6

Put the lentils in a pan with just enough water to cover and bring to the boil. Cover, turn down the heat and simmer for 15 minutes. Add the rice and just enough water to cover. Bring to the boil again, cover and simmer over low heat for 25 minutes. Keep the lid on and remove from the heat. Allow to stand for 10 minutes, then remove the lid and let the steam escape. Gently fluff up with a fork and season with a pinch of salt and 1 tablespoon of the cumin.

To make the tomato sauce, heat 2 tablespoons vegetable oil in a frying pan. Add the garlic. Simmer for 1 minute, until fragrant. Add the vinegar to the pan and bring to the boil. Add the passata, 1 teaspoon salt, the chilli powder, the remaining cumin and the sugar. Bring to the boil, then reduce the heat and simmer until you're ready to assemble.

Heat the remaining oil in a frying pan and fry the onions in 2 batches until brown and crispy. Drain on kitchen paper and keep the oil in the pan.

Bring a separate saucepan of water to the boil with 1 teaspoon salt. Cook the macaroni until tender, then drain. Stir 2 tablespoons of the onion-infused oil through the macaroni.

To construct the koshary, put a layer of rice and lentils in the bottom of a casserole dish. Add a layer of macaroni, then a layer of tomato sauce, a layer of chickpeas, then of onions. Bake it in a low oven for 20 minutes to help it bond together.

Serve with tomato sauce on the side.

FLORENCE

Florence is not where I expected to swoon over schnitzel.
To be fair, I also didn't expect the trattoria we fell into for dinner to be run by an Austrian Prince. Or for him to be so blindingly handsome that he caused me to falter while ordering. When it was suggested that the *bella principessa* might enjoy the schnitzel, it was all I could do to nod feebly in assent.

Lovers of schnitzel fall into two camps: the snug and the puffy. Those who court the snug revel in how the crust clings to the meat. It's an embrace between the hard exterior and the soft centre. Others, like me, enjoy puff, where the coating billows outwards, holding pockets of air captive next to the meat. To get a schnitzel to puff you have to make the oil dance in the pan.

For a schnitzel to shine, it should be consumed after two weeks of pasta for supper – you'll be grateful that the closest thing to a noodle on your plate are some ribbons of courgette. That said, a complimentary glass of Prosecco on the side won't tarnish the experience. Neither will some harmless flirtation with a good-looking prince.

VEAL SCHNITZEL

4 veal leg steaks,
   600–800 g/1¼–1¾ lbs.
   in total
45 g/⅓ cup self-raising
   flour
1 teaspoon salt
1 teaspoon black pepper
150 g/1½ cups dried
   breadcrumbs
1 handful flat leaf
   parsley, finely chopped
2 lemons, 1 zested, both
   cut in half
2 eggs, beaten with 1
   tablespoon cold water
vegetable oil, for
   shallow frying

Green potato salad
1 large handful flat leaf
   parsley leaves
1 large handful mint
   leaves
2 garlic cloves, crushed
180 ml/¾ cup olive oil
600 g/1¼ lbs. kipfler or
   other new potatoes
2 handfuls baby spinach
5 spring onions/scallions,
   finely diced
2 courgettes/zucchini,
   shaved into ribbons
2 tablespoons cream
   cheese

*baking sheet lined with
parchment paper*

Serves 4

Preheat the oven to 140°C (275°F) Gas 1. Put the veal between 2 pieces of greaseproof paper. Use a rolling pin to pound it to 5 mm/¼ inch thick.

Put the flour, salt and pepper on a plate. Put the breadcrumbs, parsley and lemon zest on another. Put the eggs in a bowl.

Lightly coat the veal in the flour and shake off any excess. Dip in the egg, then breadcrumbs. Place the schnitzels on a plate. Refrigerate for 30 minutes.

To make the herb dressing for the green potato salad, put the parsley, mint, garlic and olive oil in a blender and whizz until it's a lurid green slurry.

Put the potatoes in a pan of cold, salted water. Bring to the boil and cook for 10 minutes until tender. Drain and cover the pan. Rattle the pan against the lid to bang the potatoes around – roughing them up will help them absorb the dressing. Stir into the spinach, spring onions/scallions and courgettes/zucchini. Add the cream cheese and herb dressing. Stir to combine. Serve hot or warm.

To cook the schnitzel, pour 1.5 cm/½ inch oil into a frying pan. Heat over medium-high heat until the breadcrumbs sizzle when you toss them in. Reduce the heat to medium and put a schnitzel in the oil. If you like the crust to stick to the meat, cook for 2 minutes, then turn and cook for another minute. If you prefer the crust to puff, then carefully swirl the pan so the hot oil ripples over the top of the schnitzel. This should help create the steam that will help it puff. Drain the cooked schnitzel on kitchen paper. Keep it warm in the oven on the prepared baking sheet and cook the remaining schnitzels. Serve with lemon cheeks and the green potato salad.

BILBAO

Bilbao, snug in the centre of Basque territory, stands tall in my memory for two things. 1) Bilbao chorizo, a spiced semi-cured pork sausage. 2) The visual wonder of the Gaudi Guggenheim museum – a spectacle of angled turrets and wafting walls that shames all buildings sharing in its sightline.

This version of pork and beans whispers of the flavours of Spain and is visually impressive. When the whole loin is sliced family-style, it's architectural in its construction. Yet this is also a dish to call on when you want to plate individual portions nicely (possibly when you've got in-laws to impress). The softened apples and onions are a sweet and gentle base. The pork loin should adhere to rules of three and five; three slices for smaller appetites, five for hungrier souls. The chorizo nut crumble should be sprinkled over at the end – it's the real flavour hero here. Keep some extra of the chorizo crumble in your freezer for when you need to add a little artful zip to your day and just can't make it to a world-class museum.

PORK & BEANS WITH CHORIZO NUT CRUMBLE

4 red onions, cut into
   rough half moons
4 Pink Lady apples,
   peeled and cut into
   wine cork-sized chunks
3 tablespoons olive oil
1 kg/2¼ lbs. pork fillet
zest of 1 lemon
1 tablespoon butter
300 g/10 oz. green
   beans, steamed
salt and black pepper

Chorizo nut crumble
30 g/2 oz. semi-cured
   chorizo, cut up as
   small as possible
50 g/⅓ cup mixed
   hazelnuts, walnuts
   and almonds
2 garlic cloves,
   haphazardly sliced

Serves 4

Sauté the onions and apples in 2 tablespoons olive oil over low heat. Stir occasionally to prevent them sticking, and slowly cook for 30–60 minutes depending on how soft you want the apples. Add 3 tablespoons water and keep over low heat while you prepare the pork.

To make the chorizo nut crumble, put the chorizo, nuts and garlic in a small food processor. Whizz it until it's a rubble smaller than peas, but bigger than breadcrumbs.

Preheat the oven to 180°C (350°F) Gas 4. Dry the pork fillet thoroughly. Cut it into pieces that will fit lengthways in a frying pan. Season with lemon zest, salt and pepper. Heat 1 tablespoon olive oil in the frying pan until smoking. One at a time, quickly sear each piece of pork for no more than 30 seconds on each side until you have a thin brown crust. Transfer the pork pieces to a baking sheet. Dot it with pea-size pieces of butter down the length of the pork.

Cook the pork in the oven for 17–20 minutes until cooked but still slightly blushing pink in the centre. Allow to rest for 8–10 minutes before slicing into medallions.

Cook the crumble in a dry frying pan until the nuts have browned and the chorizo is cooked through.

Serve the pork with a stripe of the softened apples, with the steamed beans on the side, scattered with the chorizo nut crumble.

BERLIN
(FOR THE STURDIEST OF COMFORT FOOD)

BAKED CURRYWURST
BLACK FOREST CHEESE STRUDEL

Berlin in January is cold. It's a climate that politely but firmly requests the presence of comfort food. I'm talking rib-sticking stuff; fodder to fuel you as you trudge through thigh-deep snow on a five-hour walking tour of Teutonic architecture and public art.

If it is possible to recreate the pleasures of a winter sojourn to Berlin, it starts with *currywurst*. To an outsider, the constellation of pork sausage, ketchup and curry flavouring that makes up Berlin's favourite snack is a curious one. Yet more than 800,000 plates of sauce-doused sausage are scoffed on the streets of Berlin every year.

In my experience, a cairn of sausage slices smothered in spiced ketchup is best consumed with gloves tucked under one arm and a fistful of chips while you tut tut about people who find a holocaust memorial an appropriate location for novelty photos.

Back home, currywurst comes to the table with roast potatoes, crisp on the outside and fluffy in the centre. These are then smothered in a spiced ketchup sauce and over the top go slices of sausage and the gentle bite of sauerkraut. The cabbage is there to help with the digestion. As for the sour cream, that's just there to help gild you from the cold.

The other thing that can help protect your lily thighs is strudel. Cheese strudel is a glorious thing. It's essentially a cheesecake that's turned in on itself and walled its treasures away. Morello cherries make it even better. As for the chocolate; the Germans know better than anyone that it doesn't do any good for cocoa and cherry to be divided. Here, small nuggets of chocolate stud the unbaked strudel before melting through the curds like dark footsteps across clean paths.

This is a feast that could easily be made in a small flat in Prenzlauer Berg, in the hope that the heat from the oven will steal some of the chill away from the floor. Or it could be recreated back home, fuelling memories of some very grand and cold times while away.

BAKED CURRYWURST

12 medium roasting
    potatoes (350 g/12 oz.
    per person)
7 tablespoons olive oil
6 good Bratwurst, sliced
1 small onion, finely
    chopped
2 teaspoons sweet
    smoked paprika
3 tablespoons good
    curry powder

420 ml/1¾ cups ketchup
1½ teaspoons sugar
200 g/2 cups strained
    sauerkraut
120 ml/½ cup sour cream
    or crème fraîche
salt and black pepper

Serves 6

Preheat the oven to 220°C (425°F) Gas 7.

Wash the potatoes under cold water to get rid of any dirt. Put them in a large pan of cold salted water and bring to the boil. Simmer for 10 minutes.

Slice the potatoes into eighths, transfer to a large baking sheet and drizzle with 6 tablespoons olive oil and a good sprinkling of salt. Bake in the preheated oven for 40 minutes.

Heat 1 tablespoon olive oil in a saucepan, add the onion and sauté until translucent. Add the paprika and curry powder and cook for 30 seconds. Add the ketchup, sugar and 180 ml/ ¾ cup water and boil, uncovered, until the sauce is as thick as ordinary ketchup.

After 40 minutes of roasting the potatoes, add the Bratwurst. Bake for another 15 minutes until the potatoes are crisp and brown and the sausages are cooked through.

Serve the roasted potatoes and bratwurst with the currywurst sauce drizzled over the top and sauerkraut and sour cream on the side.

BLACK FOREST CHEESE STRUDEL

150 g/5 oz. full-fat
  ricotta, drained in
  muslin/cheesecloth
  for 1 hour
150 g/5 oz. cream cheese,
  at room temperature
3 tablespoons sugar
1 teaspoon vanilla
  extract
1 egg, beaten
4 tablespoons ground
  almonds
2 tablespoons plain/all-
  purpose flour, sifted
100 g/3½ oz. dark
  chocolate, broken into
  small squares

270 g/9 oz. (6 sheets)
  filo/phyllo pastry
50 g/3 tablespoons
  butter, melted
2 tablespoons
  breadcrumbs
680 g/1 lb. 6½ oz.
  bottled morello
  cherries, drained and
  pressed for 1 hour
icing/confectioners'
  sugar and fresh
  cherries, to serve

*baking sheet lined with
baking parchment*

damp tea towel

Serves 6

Preheat the oven to 220°C (425°F) Gas 7.

Beat the ricotta, cream cheese, sugar and vanilla with an electric mixer until smooth. Add the egg and beat well. Fold in the almonds, flour and chocolate.

Set up an assembly line with the prepared baking sheet, melted butter and filo/phyllo covered in a damp tea towel. Lay 1 sheet of pastry lengthways on the baking sheet. Brush with melted butter, top with another sheet and brush with butter. Continue until you've used all 6 sheets. Sprinkle the breadcrumbs over the top of the pastry.

Add the cheese and chocolate mixture to the pastry in a long stripe along the centre, leaving a 4-cm/1½-inch border at the top, bottom and sides. Top with the drained cherries. Fold the short ends up towards the middle and gently roll to secure. Brush the edges with melted butter and gently flip it so the seam is face down on the baking sheet.

Brush the top of the strudel with melted butter. Bake for 15 minutes, then reduce the oven temperature to 180°C (350°F) Gas 4 and bake for 20 minutes, until the pastry is golden brown.

Allow to cool for 20 minutes. Dust with icing/confectioners' sugar and serve with vanilla ice cream and fresh cherries. You can also make a sauce by reducing the juice from the cherry jar in a saucepan.

It's important to cover the pastry with the damp tea towel while you prepare this, otherwise it will become too brittle to work with. You could substitute the cherries with berries or apricots, and the dark chocolate with white chocolate.

POST CARD

CHICAGO

Asking a group of locals in Chicago where to get the best pizza invites the same kind of passionate response as openly declaring the White Sox as the superior team. Lou Malnati's was where we found our pinnacle. A Chicago pizza is no ordinary pizza. To start with, it's shaped more like a quiche and its toppings come upside down. The crust resembles flaky pastry. On top of that is a dense layer of mozzarella. The best versions shelter balls of spiced sausage, a chunky tomato sauce (which is sweetened, surprisingly, with pear), more cheese and dried herbs. All in all, it's a piping-hot pile of sweet and spicy dairy, tomato and meat. It's somewhat light on structural integrity when the walls are breached, but gruntingly strong in flavour. It's best eaten with a knife and fork, a cold beer and a firm plan to go and do some exercise somewhere the next day.

DEEP-DISH MEATBALL PIZZA PIE

Pizza dough
¼ tablespoon fast-action/active dry yeast
¼ tablespoon sugar
60 g/¼ cup clarified butter or shortening
260 g/2 cups plain/all-purpose flour
salt

Sauce & meatballs
1 onion, finely chopped
2 tablespoons olive oil
2 garlic cloves, thinly sliced
1 x 400-g/14-oz. can tomatoes

1 pear, peeled, cored and chopped into small pieces
1 big teaspoon dried oregano
1 bay leaf
450 g/1 lb. beef meatballs
300 g/10½ oz. fresh mozzarella, patted dry
3 tablespoons grated Parmesan

non-stick 20-cm/8-inch loose-bottomed cake pan

Serves 4, with a large green salad

Mix 175 ml/¾ cup water with the yeast and sugar and leave for 5 minutes. Put the yeast mixture, butter or shortening, 130 g/1 cup flour and a pinch of salt in an electric mixer with a dough hook and mix for 5 minutes. Add 100 g/¾ cup more flour and mix until a dough forms. Add the remaining flour if needed.

The dough should be wet, but shouldn't stick to your hands. Put the dough in a covered bowl in the fridge to rise overnight. Remove 2–3 hours before use.

To make the sauce, lightly sauté the onion in a heavy-based casserole dish with the olive oil and garlic. When the onion is translucent and soft, add the tomato, pear pieces, oregano and bay leaf. Cook slowly for 1 hour, stirring occasionally, until the pear has dissolved into the tomato. Remove the bay leaf. Blitz with a stick blender until smooth.

Assemble the pizza

Preheat the oven to its highest setting. Brown the meatballs in a frying pan and add them to the tomato sauce. Pat out the dough in the cake pan, and up the sides. Make sure you pat the dough firmly all around the edge using your knuckles. Place three-quarters of the mozzarella in the bottom of the pan. Cover with the meatballs and tomato. Top with the remaining mozzarella and the Parmesan. Bake for 25–30 minutes until the crust is puffed and golden. If the inside is still at all soupy, return to the oven for another 5–10 minutes.

To serve, remove the sides of the cake pan and cut into quarters with a large knife or cake server.

BEAUNE

The local apéritif of the walled French city of Beaune is a stealthy thing.

A *communard* is a dark twist on a Kir, melding red wine with blackcurrant liqueur. If you're not careful, it'll knock you off your chair before you've even had a chance to settle in. For a much safer way to consume the local French Burgundy, combine it with braised beef, mushrooms, lardons and carrots and leave them to get acquainted in the oven for a few hours. Although if you were looking for a heightened taste of Beaune, you could always give this classic stew the *communard* treatment and add a kick of the cassis liqueur to the pot.

One option is to serve these silken hunks of meat over mashed potato or white bean purée. Or you could do what every homesick Australian does when stranded in the middle of France, and ponder how it would taste under a cap of pastry. Experience tells me that most good stews are even better when gussied up as a pie. This is just another example. Mushy peas and tomato sauce on the side are optional.

BEEF BOURGUIGNON PIE

1 kg/2¼ lbs. beef shin or chuck steak, cubed
1½ tablespoons plain/all-purpose flour
1 teaspoon salt
1 teaspoon black pepper
3 tablespoons olive oil
2 carrots, diced
3 garlic cloves, crushed
2 onions, diced
2 bay leaves
675 ml/2¾ cups red wine (Burgundy is classic)
2 tablespoons tomato purée/paste
1 teaspoon sugar
2 tablespoons cassis or sherry (optional)
150 g/5 oz. lardons/streaky bacon, cut into strips
200 g/6½ oz. button mushrooms, halved
375 g/12½ oz. puff pastry
1 egg, beaten

4 ovenproof bowls or pudding containers

Serves 4

Preheat the oven to 230°C (450°F) Gas 8. Dust the beef in the flour, salt and pepper.

Heat 1 tablespoon olive oil in a casserole dish over high heat, and brown half of the meat. Remove and add another tablespoon of oil before browning the other half (try not to crowd the pan – you don't want the meat to stew).

Remove the meat and add 1 tablespoon olive oil to the pan. Sauté the carrots, garlic and onions until the onion is translucent.

Return the meat to the pan. Add the bay leaves and red wine. Scrape up the sediment on the bottom of the pan with a spoon and encourage it to join the stew. This is where the flavour is.

Simmer over low heat with the lid off for 2 hours, or longer if you have it. An hour before serving, add the tomato purée/paste and sugar. (If you feel inclined, add the cassis or sherry.)

Just before serving, brown the lardons in a frying pan. Add the mushrooms and fry them in the fat that's been rendered from the lardons. Add both to the beef stew. Season with salt and pepper.

Divide the stew among 4 pie dishes. Divide the pastry into 4, roll out on a lightly floured surface and place on top of the pies. Seal around the edges of the dishes. Brush with beaten egg, make a cut in the centre and bake for 25–30 minutes, until golden.

SAN FRANCISCO

Soup pie. Crazier things have been suggested on the coast of California. As a city, San Francisco does soup well, particularly if glossed with cream.

A helping of chowder in a sourdough bowl by the Fisherman's Wharf is as much a rite of passage in the city as an espresso at Bluebottle, a taco from The Mission or a scoop of Bi-Rite ice cream.

There is a logic that says a steaming bowl of soup cries for nothing more than a bark of texture to swipe through it. Toast, quesadillas, crackers all have merit. So does a pastry lid that will plume over the bowl of soup while they're baked. We ate one version of this at Bistro Jeanty in San Francisco. This iteration dials down the cream and adds a few other elements. One is pressing herbs into the undercarriage of the pastry; I like basil. Another is crumbling some cheese into the centre of the soup; I like goat. What still remains is the novelty from the heat of the soup in the oven puffing the pastry up to a dome.

When you crack open the bridge of pastry the soup will steam up like an atmospheric fog. If that doesn't remind you of time spent in San Francisco, then I don't know what will.

TOMATO SOUP PIE

1 tablespoon butter
1 tablespoon olive oil
2 onions, thinly sliced
   into half moons
3 garlic cloves
1 bay leaf
3 peppercorns
3 tablespoons tomato
   purée/paste
500 g/1 lb. 2 oz. ripe
   tomatoes, peeled,
   seeded and chopped

125 ml/½ cup double/
   heavy cream
2 tablespoons goats'
   cheese
275 g/9 oz. puff pastry
1 egg, beaten
2 handfuls basil leaves

stick blender
4 deep pie dishes

Serves 2 for a main/
entrée, or 4 for starter/
appetizer

Melt the butter and olive oil in a heavy-based pan. Sauté the onions, garlic, bay leaf and peppercorns for 10 minutes, just until the onions have softened.

Add the tomato purée/paste and turn the heat up to combine the tomato paste with the onions.

Add the tomatoes. Simmer with the lid on for 40 minutes, stirring occasionally to prevent the onions and tomatoes catching on the bottom. Cook until the tomatoes have started breaking down and the onions are soft.

Preheat the oven to 230°C (450°F) Gas 8. Remove the bay leaf, then purée the tomatoes and onions with a stick blender. Add the cream and blitz until smooth (for extra smooth, pass it through a strainer).

Season with salt and pepper and divide among the pie dishes. The soup should be lukewarm by now (or you can make it ahead of time). Top each bowl of soup with crumbled goats' cheese.

Roll out and cut the puff pastry into 4 squares, allowing some overhang over the pie dishes. Brush the pastry with beaten egg, then layer 4 basil leaves over it. Brush the top of the leaves with egg to secure them. Affix it carefully, with the basil facing down, to the top of the pie dish – don't let the soup touch the pastry. Pull it as tight as you can, like a drum, and fold it over the bowl with hospital corners at the side so that it fits tightly over the soup.

Carefully brush the top of the pastry with beaten egg and add 1 or 2 more basil leaves to the top.

Bake for 15 minutes, until the pastry is puffed and golden. To serve, crack open a circle in the top of the pastry and peel it back. Drop extra basil leaves in the void.

SNOW PLAY
(FROM THREDBO TO ZERMATT)

SHEPHERDS' PIES WITH POTATO SCALES

APPLE & ROSEMARY FRITTERS

Some skiing jaunts are all about towns where the local transport is by electric buggy and horse-drawn carts, and where fresh cakes are left out for you each afternoon. Others involve negotiations for a weekly menu for six over email, late-night shopping trips and a five-hour drive in a crammed car from Sydney to the Australian Alps.

There are some essential items for a successful self-catered ski trip: fun-sized chocolate bars that will get forgotten in one of the 12 pockets of your technical gear. Sunscreen. Gin. And meals that are swift to pull together, warming and light on starchy carbohydrates (because goodness knows you'll eat enough of those on the slopes while muttering about how your boots don't quite fit).

A traditional shepherds' pie is the ultimate in thrifty comfort food. In its classic form it consists of leftover roast lamb or mutton and gravy caught under a snowy dome of mashed potato (cheesy crust optional). This is a loose interpretation. The first version, in Thredbo, contained kangaroo mince. It was a compromise for a motley group that included two environmentally motivated pescaterians (consuming half of the Australian crest deemed permissible on sustainability grounds). Here, the bulk of the mash came not from potato, but puréed white beans: a lighter and swifter topping. The thin scales of potato over the top add a nice layer of crunch. Over time it has morphed into a staple meal to make in bulk, freeze until you need it, then throw in the oven while you make a gin and tonic and join five people hunching over the same piste map.

We found the other kind of skiing high in the Swiss Alps. Zermatt is a watercolour picture of a European snow fantasy. The small streets of the town are decked with twinkly lights and hoods are lined with fur. Up on the slopes, halfway down the blue run number 6 from Sunnega Express, is Chez Vrony. Skis are parked at the front of the gate in a chaotic crèche. There are lambskin covers on sloped chairs and the view is straight towards the Toblerone peaks of the Matterhorn (it's bigger than at Disneyland, I promise). This was the first place I tasted apple fritters.

Apple fritters are the love-child of a donut and an apple pie, and their texture is equivalent to burying down under flannel sheets at the close of a cold day. They're perfect snow food, and not just because the blizzard of rosemary sugar over the top recalls the sight of pine needles pricking out from fields of white. The only other thing they need is a puddle of melting ice cream.

It's the kind of dessert you crave when you've spent the afternoon hauling yourself on metal sticks over improbably slippery surfaces.

Eat both of these while snow falls like silence and you gingerly massage your aching shins.

SHEPHERDS' PIES WITH POTATO SCALES

3 tablespoons olive oil
1 onion, diced
3 carrots, diced
500 g/1 lb. 2 oz. minced/ground lamb (or beef if you prefer)
2 garlic cloves
2 tablespoons tomato purée/paste
250 ml/1 cup red wine
1 tablespoon Worcestershire sauce
1 bay leaf
2 x 400-g/14-oz. cans white beans (any will do), drained
125 ml/½ cup milk
1 handful flat leaf parsley, finely chopped
8–10 new potatoes, halved and cut into thin slices
salt and black pepper
green salad, to serve

1 large pie dish or 4 individual pie dishes

Serves 4

APPLE & ROSEMARY FRITTERS

2 eggs
125 ml/½ cup milk
130 g/1 cup self-raising
  flour
2 tablespoons white
  sugar
½ teaspoon salt
750 ml/3 cups oil for
  deep-frying

5 Pink Lady or Granny
  Smith apples, cut into
  discs 1-cm/½-inch
  thick, core removed
50 g/¼ cup sugar
3 teaspoons rosemary,
  finely chopped
whipped cream or ice
  cream, to serve

Serves 4–6

Preheat the oven to 200°C (400°F) Gas 6.

Heat 1 tablespoon olive oil in a casserole dish and sauté the onions and carrots over medium heat until the onions are translucent. Turn up the heat, add the mince and brown it well.

Add the garlic, tomato purée/paste, red wine, Worcestershire sauce and bay leaf. Reduce the heat to medium and simmer for 40 minutes, then season well with salt and pepper (don't be shy).

To make the 'mash', combine the milk with the drained beans. Use a stick blender to whizz until smooth. Fold in the parsley and season with salt and pepper.

Divide the mixture between the 4 pie dishes. Top with the white bean 'mash', then arrange the thin slices of potato on top so they stick up like armour on a triceratops. Drizzle olive oil over the top and season with a pinch of salt. Bake for 40 minutes until the potato scales are crisp.

Serve with extra Worcestershire sauce and a green salad.

Beat together the eggs and milk. Sift in the flour, sugar and salt. Stir until smooth. If you can, let the batter rest for an hour or so, or longer.

Heat the oil to 190°C (375°F) in a deep-fat fryer or deep heavy-based pan.

Dip the apple slices in the batter and deep-fry a few at a time, turning once, until puffed and golden. Drain on kitchen paper.

Whizz the rosemary and the sugar together in a blender until the rosemary is blitzed into small pieces and well combined through the sugar.

Dust the fritters with the rosemary sugar and serve with whipped cream or ice cream.

The Sweet Stuff

DESSERTS FOR SHARING,
TREATS FOR SNEAKING
& THINGS TO CALL ON
WHEN A GREY DAY
NEEDS A LIFT

NEW YORK

This treat treads a fine line between a drink and dessert. It's childhood comfort nestled in a glass. It's the taste of fire-touched marshmallows and quickly dripping ice cream. It's what you turn to when the world is just a little too shiny and sharp.

Over the course of 12 hours in the Big Apple we'd been chased by a waitress and admonished on the street for miscalculating a tip (we quickly learnt that 12.5% just won't float in the city of dreams). I'd been shoved on the subway and scorched by the summer sun. When I stumbled into The Stand, I was just seeking a burger and some air conditioning. And then we saw the shakes.

Two sips into a toasted marshmallow shake and the world was a sweet place again. 'You know the only thing that could make me more relaxed?' my previously harried husband said to me. 'If this had a shot of something.' As with so many things, he was right.

TOASTED MARSHMALLOW THICKSHAKES

8 marshmallows
3 tablespoons milk
2 tablespoons natural yogurt
3 scoops good vanilla
  ice cream
1–2 shots brandy or vodka
  (optional)
whipped cream and shaved
  chocolate, for decoration

stick blender

Serves 1

Toast the marshmallows in a pan under the grill/broiler, turning until each side is burnished.

Put the milk, yogurt, ice cream and 6 of the toasted marshmallows in a blender, or in a bowl that can take a stick blender.

Add the booze now, if that's what you need in your life (no judgement).

Pour the shake into a glass, garnish with 2 more toasted marshmallows and, if you like, whipped cream and shaved chocolate (also no judgement).

CAMBRIDGE

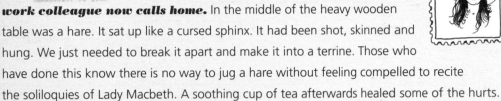

I first prepared jugged hare at an estate in Cambridge that an old work colleague now calls home. In the middle of the heavy wooden table was a hare. It sat up like a cursed sphinx. It had been shot, skinned and hung. We just needed to break it apart and make it into a terrine. Those who have done this know there is no way to jug a hare without feeling compelled to recite the soliloquies of Lady Macbeth. A soothing cup of tea afterwards healed some of the hurts.

Despite their gentle appearance, these tea-scented panna cottas also require some forceful work with a (clean) blade before serving. Making them in plastic cups avoids the problems of extracting them from the moulds. Once they have set, simply upend and plunge a knife into the top, breaking the vacuum seal, then watch them gently morph down onto the plate. We served them with salted dates and toasted almonds. There was sweet, salt and crunch, held against the softness of cooked cream and milk. It was almost enough to make us forget the trauma of the hare. Almost, but not quite.

EARL GREY PANNA COTTA WITH SALTED DATE PURÉE

Panna cotta
3 gelatine leaves
250 ml/1 cup milk
250 ml/1 cup double/ heavy cream
2 Earl Grey tea bags
25 g/1 oz. sugar
125 g/1 cup flaked/ slivered almonds, toasted or roasted

Salted date purée
125 g/1 cup pitted dates
pinch of bicarbonate of soda/baking soda
3 tablespoons sherry
½ tablespoon sea salt flakes

4 plastic cups (wipe the insides with a little bit of vegetable oil)

Serves 4

Soak the gelatine leaves in a little cold water until they're slimy and limpid to the touch.

Put the milk, cream, tea bags and sugar in a pan and bring to a simmer. Remove the tea bags when the mixture has turned fawn coloured.

Give the gelatine leaves a good squeeze, then add them to the warm milk mixture. Stir until the gelatine has dissolved.

Pour the mixture into the plastic cups. Let them cool, then place them in the fridge for 4–6 hours until completely set. Upend the plastic cups, one on each plate. Puncture the top of the cups with the tip of a knife. This will allow air in and the suction seal to break, releasing the panna cottas.

To make the salted date purée, put the dates in a pan with 180 ml/¾ cup boiling water and the bicarbonate of soda/baking soda. Simmer, stirring occasionally, so the dates break down into a sludgy purée, then add the sherry, and salt to taste.

Spoon the date purée next to the panna cottas and sprinkle the roasted almonds over the top.

Instead of the salted dates and almonds, a compote of apples, pears and lemon juice on the side with toasted pine nuts would be another way to highlight the flavours in the tea.

LONDON FIELDS

Socks and sandals. Pale legs peeking out from shorts. Crowded pub courtyards and sticky jugs of Pimms. Elderflower cakes eaten on musty picnic rugs. If the promise of an English summer had a taste, it might be this. Elderflowers are in season in the UK from May onwards (but the cordial they steep in is available all year round). Elderflower may remind some people of the inside of their grandmother's bureau, but its nectared sweetness transports me to lazy walks home from school in summer, sucking on star jasmine stems. Joining in with the elderflowers are fresh berries, as cheap as a laugh and oozing with sweet juice. From there it's easy. Make a cake flavoured with almonds. Split it in half. Spread it with sweetened cream cheese frosting, dot with berries, then sandwich the top on and repeat. If you're feeling very optimistic about the sunshine, transfer the cake back into its tin, wrap with parchment and tote to a picnic spot in London Fields. If both hope and the weather fail you, it eats just as well on a carpet picnic inside your flat.

ELDERFLOWER ALMOND CAKE WITH SUMMER BERRIES

Cake
175 g/1½ sticks softened butter
175 g/generous ¾ cup caster/superfine sugar
4 eggs
150 g/generous 1 cup self-raising flour, sifted
150 g/¾ cup ground almonds
4 tablespoons elderflower cordial (or St Germain liqueur)

Cream cheese frosting
300 g/10 oz. cream cheese
5 tablespoons icing/confectioners' sugar
2 tablespoons elderflower cordial
300 g/10 oz. fresh berries (such as raspberries, blackberries or blueberries)

23-cm/9-inch springform cake pan, greased and lined with baking parchment

Serves 8

Preheat the oven to 160°C (320°F) Gas 3.

Beat the butter and sugar until light and fluffy. Add the eggs one at a time, whisking well between each one. Add the flour and almonds and fold in gently. Transfer to the cake pan and bake. Check on the cake after 45 minutes, then cover with foil; this will help prevent it getting too brown. Bake for 1 hour in total, or until golden and a skewer comes out clean. Allow to cool in the pan for 15 minutes, then remove from the pan.

Carefully cut the cake in half and brush the elderflower cordial over the sliced side of each half.

To make the frosting, beat together the cream cheese, icing/confectioners' sugar and elderflower cordial. Spread two-thirds of the frosting in the centre of the cake. Add half the berries and sandwich the top on the cake. Gently spread the remaining frosting over the top of the cake and add the remaining berries. If you're serving this to adults you can substitute St Germain elderflower liqueur.

PLANE FOOD

It is a necessary evil that to get to places of interest you may have to fly.
There's a state of suspension that's specific to being 37,000 feet up.

It's a place where grown men will sob when dogs die on tiny screens. A place where long socks become sartorially acceptable. And a place where long-held dining standards plummet.

Three hours into a 24-hour commute, the jangle and bash of metal carts down meanly carpeted aisles carries the same excitement as an ice-cream van playing *Greensleeves*. Anything to break the monotony of breathing loud, too-cold air.

Seasoned fliers among us may swap surprising tales of the quality of Korean Airlines' *bibimbap*, and bento-esque fare in square packs on Japan Airlines. But fables of travel food are more often made of darker stuff. They're about the kraken-like stench of 200 packets of dried shrimp simultaneously opened during snack time on Dragon Air. Of collective indigestion of vegetarians who endure 28 hours of carbohydrates smudged in red sauce; not *puttanesca* or *patatas bravas*, more crime-scenes painted on pale pastes. The highlight for me has been breakfast aboard Rossiya Airlines: two flabby Berliner sausages and three cubes of powder compressed into potato. On top of all that, there are the physical limitations of eating up here to surmount: feeble knives and dinky pouches of dressing which will unfailingly spurt down the front of your shirt when opened. And then there's the simple issue of taste. The lack of moisture in a pressurized cabin can shoulder a degree of responsibility for the bland duvets of flavour on offer. But the real culprit is the container. You wouldn't eat from it on the ground, unless you were institutionalized to some degree. So there's one solution to avoid the trauma. Don't peel back the foil.

Surely there has to be a better way? Beyond swallowing a Temazepam and a glass of red wine, this is the best I can offer for long-haul flights (economy style). If you're flying at the front of the plane, with cutlery, crockery and the finest of linens, move on and enjoy your Champagne and caviar. There's very little for you here.

1) Be organized.

Arrive at the airport with plenty of time for a smug drink and a meal somewhere on the other side of security. That way you'll be a chooser, not a beggar, when you get up on the plane. Nine times out of ten you'll find a faux Parisian bistro where you can consume an average *steak frites*, encircled by harried suits having a pre-flight date with their Blackberry. But it's always worth looking around for other options. You may, for instance, happen upon an excellent Mexican restaurant tucked up a flight of stairs if you bother to investigate. I can assure you that after you've drunk a margarita as big as your head you won't worry so much that your flight from McCarran to JFK has just been delayed by another four hours.

2) *Think outside the square.*

There is nothing like the healing sting of the first gin and tonic on a plane. But after that, think outside the parameters of the foil box. Drinks are not just drinks. Consider tomato juice, a standard offering in an inflight Bloody Mary mix, as a weaker cousin of gazpacho. Add a dash of Tabasco and two tinkling cubes of ice to the plastic cup. Let them meld for a few minutes. Then sip and pretend you're already sunning yourself somewhere on the Costa Brava.

3) *Pimp your roll.*

Even the saddest of in-flight fodder will usually come accompanied by a domed bread roll and a pat of butter. Don't just shuffle the carbohydrates to the side. Use them to your advantage. For morning flights, sneak three squares of good-quality dark chocolate into your pocket. Add a pinch of salt, or, more controversially, a smear of jam or marmalade. Let it rest on top of the hot foil

for three minutes to relax. Then imagine it's stuffed brioche or a chocolate croissant. For lunchtime or evening flights, turn to cured meats as your saviour. Pack three slices of sinfully good *jamón* or a few aggressively spiced circles of salami. If the pig is good enough, the bread can serve as bulk.

4) *Use your lemons.*

If you must open the foil packet, think about asking for two extra wedges of lemon with your first gin and tonic. Plane food is lacking in many things, acidity chief among them. So if the trip is long, the in-flight entertainment fails and hunger scratches hard, choose wisely. Choose beef over chicken and chicken over fish. Add a squeeze of lemon and a sprinkle of pepper. Then shut your eyes and eat, all the while getting more and more excited about the sterling things you'll scoff as soon as you're back on solid ground.

FRANGELICO AFFOGATO

500 g/1 pint good vanilla
   ice cream
100 ml/3½ oz. Frangelico
4 shots espresso
40 g/1½ oz. good dark
   chocolate, grated

espresso machine
4 chilled glasses

Serves 4

Divide the ice cream between
4 chilled glasses.
   Pour a shot of espresso and a
shot of Frangelico over each portion.
   Top with shards of chocolate.

BOLOGNA

A city can mean different things to different people. For some, Bologna is about the sweet joy of devouring tortellini, the cowboy hat-shaped parcels of filled pasta the city is famed for. For others, it is placed on a travel itinerary for one singular purpose: the Ducati motorbike factory. Finding a compromise between a contented long lunch and a trek to see machines can be a rocky path. It's in instances like this that quick desserts are everything. An affogato carves a middle road for when you don't know whether to serve coffee, dessert, or a post-dinner tipple. As I learnt at the Ducati factory, for things of quality, the materials can be everything. Don't scrimp on the espresso beans, the ice cream, or the dark chocolate. If your spouse had no choice but to leave the toy of their dreams in a showroom on the other side of the world, feel free to let them drown their ice cream and sorrows in hazelnut liqueur as well as espresso. If not (and particularly if they're riding home) – go easy.

APRICOT FRANGIPANE PUDDINGS

110 g/7½ tablespoons
    butter at room
    temperature
3 tablespoons plain/
    all-purpose flour,
    plus extra for dusting
450 g/1 lb. apricot flesh
    (about 10 stoned/
    pitted apricots),
50 g/¼ cup brown/
    muscovado sugar

110 g/½ cup sugar
2 large eggs, beaten
130 g/⅔ cup ground
    almonds
ice cream, to serve
icing/confectioners'
    sugar, for dusting

*6 ramekins, greased and
dusted with flour*

Serves 6

Preheat the oven to 180°C (350°F) Gas 4.

Cut the apricots into quarters and simmer in a pan with the brown sugar and 1 tablespoon water for 3 minutes. Arrange the apricots over the bottom of the ramekins.

Cream the butter and sugar until duckling yellow and fluffy, then beat in the eggs one at a time. Carefully fold in the almonds and flour, then spoon the mixture over the apricots.

Bake in the preheated oven for 30 minutes. Remove from the oven, cool for 5 minutes, then turn out onto 4 serving plates, ensuring that all of the fruit tumbles out to sit on top of the frangipane.

Dust with icing/confectioners' sugar and serve with ice cream.

VAL D'ISERE

If there's a more noxious moniker in English lexicon than 'chalet girl', I don't know it. With that in mind, the first iteration of these puddings was taught to me by the 'twenty-something woman who prepared our meals, changed our towels and hosted us in a bed-and-breakfast-style arrangement in the French Alps'. She and her partner were roaring delights, even more so on the nights they would come and sit at the table and share a bottle of wine. Her original frangipane puddings were topped with sliced apples, although after toying with the recipe I find stone fruits provide a pleasing twang to cut through the richness of the almonds. All you really need for a frangipane is butter, sugar, eggs and ground almonds, though a small amount of flour helps give these upside-down puddings a bit more structural integrity. If you prepare them up to the baking stage earlier in the day, they'll give you a good amount of breathing space when entertaining. Pop them in the oven and then go and have a glass of wine by the fire with your friends. You can turn them out yourself and plate them nicely, or you could get everyone to muck in and do their own. The only thing that's non-negotiable is ice cream, to melt like pooling snow over the pudding's craggy tops.

IOWA

The roads that link California and Chicago are long and straight, and the states they traverse are square.

Three days into a road trip, I had turfed out our aspirational talking tapes and abandoned hopes of educational improvement while driving. I passed the time singing rock ballads (The Eagles and Sting, mainly) and researching one thing. I couldn't take it easy until I found more pie. Pie was what sustained me, past Iowa's fields of gold and Nebraska's mini malls. The pinnacle was peach pie, à la mode. Flaky pastry was key, and a balance of fruit to mildly tart sauce; the mild squash where the filling nestled into the base. In between pit stops I scratched around for what might improve the experience. The only thing I could call forth was berries.

Peach Melba is a classic combination of peaches and raspberries, created by Escoffier in honour of Dame Nellie Melba, an Australian with a far more pleasing voice than mine. The resulting pie, made months later, is one worth singing about. Sweet but perky, the raspberries slump against the peaches as they cook. And yes, for those with keen eyes, that *is* vodka in the crust. It might be there because vodka chills harder than water, ensuring the flakiest crust you'll find across 50 states. Or because the memory of five days in a small car with my singing are enough to drive anyone to the bottle.

PEACH MELBA PIE

Pastry
- 250 g/2 cups plain/all-purpose flour, plus extra for dusting
- 50 g/scant ½ cup icing/confectioners' sugar
- 125 g/1 stick butter, frozen and grated onto a cold plate
- 3 tablespoons very cold vodka
- 2 eggs, beaten
- milk and sugar, to finish

Filling
- 450 g/1 lb. peach slices (about 4 peaches)
- 250 g/2 cups fresh raspberries, or drained frozen
- 50 g/¼ cup sugar
- 30 g/¼ cup plain/all-purpose flour
- 25 g/¼ cup cornflour/cornstarch
- 2 teaspoons lemon juice
- pinch of salt

20-cm/8-inch pie dish, greased baking beans/pie weights

Serves 4–6

To make the pastry, sift the flour and sugar together into a large bowl. Run your hands under very cold water and dry them well. Use your fingertips to work the butter into the flour until it looks like crumbs. Add 1 beaten egg and the vodka and mix with your hands until the dough just comes together. Wrap in clingfilm/plastic wrap and refrigerate for 30 minutes.

Preheat the oven to 200°C (400°F) Gas 6. Dust a work surface with flour. Divide the pastry into two. Wrap and return the second half to the fridge. Roll the first half out to 5 mm/¼ inch thick. Roll it around the rolling pin and drape it into the prepared pie dish. Ease it in, leaving an overhang. Prick with a fork and add the baking beans/ pie weights. Bake for 10 minutes, then remove the beans. Brush with some of the second egg and bake for another 10 minutes until light brown.

For the filling, skin the peaches by scoring a cross in the top, then dipping in boiling water for 30 seconds. Transfer to iced water; the skins should slip off. Remove the stones and slice the peaches. Combine them with the remaining ingredients, then transfer to the pie casing.

Roll out the second half of the pastry to a circle 25 cm/10 inches in diameter. Lay over the pie and crimp the edges. Seal with more beaten egg. Make three 5-cm/2-inch slits in the centre to allow the steam to escape. Brush the top with beaten egg and sprinkle with sugar. Bake for 45 minutes until the pastry is golden.

A TALE OF TWO CHRISTMASES
SYDNEY (HOT)

My stories of Christmas past involve carols by candlelight in a bush amphitheatre, beneath the wide eyes of ringtail possums. Santa would arrive wearing board shorts and sunglasses to avoid the 8.00pm glare of the sun. After we'd sung the carol of the birds, we'd march home through streets lined by eucalyptus trees strung with coloured lights. We'd linger with a bowl of ice cream before being shuttled off to bed so that our parents could wrap presents in peace.

As we got older, Christmas Eve involved other iced delights: frozen berry daiquiris, sipped while swatting mosquitos and dangling our feet in the shallows of a salt-water swimming pool.

A hot Christmas celebration calls for things that can be easily made ahead and kept at room temperature, or swiftly plucked from the barbecue or freezer just prior to serving.

Our last hot Christmas involved seven nieces and nephews under four, their elbows knocking against our legs as we plucked things from a buffet. The few nods to a traditional European Christmas were found in the colour scheme. Red, green and white are all present. Our feast began with a large platter of shaved asparagus, *ricotta salata* (salted ricotta), pistachios and cherries – all of which play in a similar key of sweetness. It continued with a grand barbecued fish. Tranches of a plump pink ocean trout cuddled up to spoonfuls of caponata, a robust Sicilian aubergine/eggplant and pepper stew with nuts, currants, capers and a little bit of chocolate. For what is a proper celebration without the promise of chocolate?

When Christmas can occasionally reach 40°C/104°F, there's no place for piping-hot desserts. Dessert was an ice cream terrine, with a chocolate sauce as boozy as we dared.

You could make the Christmas pudding that gets trampled through ice cream, judiciously feeding the bowl with nips of brandy each night before bed. Or if you're lucky as we are, you'll be given a perfect one each year from an honorary member of the family.

This is a no-fuss feast that leaves plenty of time to do more important things. Like taking a dunk in a swimming pool and sipping a cocktail while salt water trickles down your back. To me, there's no finer way to raise a toast to the joy that comes from the Christmas present.

ASPARAGUS, CHERRY & SALTED RICOTTA SALAD

3 bunches asparagus
zest and juice of ½ lemon
4 tablespoons good olive oil
3 courgettes/zucchini, shaved
**   into ribbons**
150 g/1 cup cherries, pitted
2 tablespoons shelled pistachios
240 g/1 cup ricotta salata
salt and black pepper

Serves 6

Steam or grill/broil the asparagus until cooked, but still with a little bite. Lay the asparagus along a serving platter.

Make a dressing with the lemon zest and juice and olive oil. Use your hands to toss the dressing through the courgette/zucchini ribbons. Drape the ribbons over the top of the asparagus. Halve the cherries.

Top with the cherries, pistachios and crumbled ricotta salata. Season well with salt and pepper.

Ricotta salata is salted, dried ricotta. If you can't find it, add 1 teaspoon salt to good-quality fresh ricotta and allow it to drain in a strainer for 2 hours before serving.

SPICED CAPONATA

150 ml/⅔ cup olive oil
2 red onions, sliced into thin
    half moons
1 fennel bulb or 4 celery stalks,
    finely diced
2 red peppers, deseeded and diced
2 large aubergines/eggplants, diced
½ teaspoon salt
1 x 400-g/14-oz. can plum tomatoes
zest of ½ orange
30 g/1 oz. dark chocolate
piece of fresh ginger the size of a
    wine cork, grated

2 tablespoons currants

2 tablespoons sugar, or to taste

2 tablespoons capers, drained

2–4 tablespoons good red wine vinegar

50 g/⅓ cup pine nuts, toasted

50 g/½ cup flaked/ slivered almonds, toasted

1 large handful flat leaf parsley

Heat the oil in a large casserole dish over medium heat. Add the onions, fennel, red pepper, aubergines/ eggplants and salt, and sweat over high heat for at least 25 minutes, or until very tender. Stir frequently to prevent it catching on the bottom of the pan.

Add the tomatoes, orange zest, dark chocolate, ginger, currants and sugar and allow to simmer on a medium heat for 15 minutes.

Add the capers, then the vinegar, tablespoon by tablespoon, stirring and tasting before adding each additional spoon. Stop when you reach a good balance of sweet and acidic. If you've gone too far, you can add a little more sugar.

Season with salt and pepper, top with toasted nuts and flat leaf parsley. Serve at room temperature.

STUFFED SALMON WITH SPICED CAPONATA

1 x 2.5-kg/6-lb. whole salmon or ocean trout, gutted and scaled
2 lemons, sliced
1 handful flat leaf parsley
1 fennel bulb, thinly sliced
1 tablespoon butter

Minted yogurt
360 ml/1½ cups Greek yogurt
2 tablespoons olive oil
1 teaspoon salt
1 handful mint leaves, finely chopped

barbecue
kitchen string

Serves 6

Heat the barbecue until the temperature reaches 180°C (350°F). Dry the fish well with kitchen paper and ensure the belly is clean. Put the lemon slices, parsley and fennel in the belly of the fish. Use the kitchen string to create loops and tie the fish shut at 2 intervals so that the filling doesn't escape.

Rub a large piece of foil with butter to help prevent the fish from sticking. Wrap the fish in the foil and place on the barbecue. Cook for 20 minutes, then gently turn and cook for another 15–20 minutes until an instant-read thermometer inserted in the thickest part of the fish registers 57°C (135°F). Remove the fish from the grill and gently remove the foil. Allow the fish to cool for 5 minutes, then remove the string and serve with the caponata and minted yogurt.

Minted yogurt

Put the yogurt, olive oil, salt and mint leaves in a bowl and whisk to combine.

CHRISTMAS PUDDING SEMIFREDDO WITH BOOZY CHOCOLATE SAUCE

1 litre/1 quart good vanilla ice cream
vegetable oil, for greasing
400 g/14 oz. Christmas pudding
zest of ½ orange

Boozy chocolate sauce
250 ml/1 cup double/heavy cream
3 tablespoons brandy
3 tablespoons light brown sugar
pinch of salt
150 g/5 oz. dark chocolate, finely chopped

20 x 12.5-cm/8 x 5-inch loaf pan, greased

Serves 6

Soften the ice cream in the fridge for about 30–40 minutes until it will scoop easily. Grease the inside of the loaf pan with a little vegetable oil, then line it with clingfilm/plastic wrap. Break the Christmas pudding into coin-sized pieces. Combine the rubble of the pudding, softened ice cream and orange zest. Transfer the mixture to the loaf pan and cover with clingfilm. Refreeze.

To make the chocolate sauce, put the cream, brandy, sugar and salt in a pan and bring to the boil. Put the chocolate in a heatproof bowl and pour the hot mixture over the top. Whisk until combined. Serve the hot sauce with the cold semifreddo.

LONDON (COLD)

CHRISTMAS CARPACCIO

STUFFED PORK WITH
ROAST PEAR SAUCE

MINCE PIES WITH
EGGNOG CUSTARD

Eggnog. That's what The Hungry One requested after he hauled the six-foot pine back home over sleet and circles of black ice. During our first English Christmas, Borough was blanketed in snow. Earlier that day we'd ventured to the market in our ski pants. We thought that's what you wore when flakes of frost fell from the sky. We now realize how silly we must have looked.

To celebrate the season we invited friends to the flat. We decorated the tree with garlands crafted from burly red wool and shiny gold caramels. We drank Champagne that had chilled in a snowdrift on the balcony and told stories of Christmas past. The feast we sat down to started with a carpaccio of sea bass, dotted with pomegranate seeds and the Scandinavian lilt of dill and horseradish. While Tiny Tim may have dreamed of goose, our main event was roast pork. It was stuffed and rolled with citrus and dried fruits, distended like a stocking full of presents intended for an exceptionally well-behaved child.

It may have been the sensation of hosting our first adult Christmas that made us revert to such giddy glee. It may have been the Champagne. But we all swear we saw it. After we cut open the pleats of crackling, there, in the stuffing, was Santa. Like Abraham Lincoln in potato crisps/chips and Jesus in toast, he was there. He had cranberries for eyes and his smile was sage.

Dessert was a more low-key affair. The concept of eggnog, a frankendrink that combines the fluffiness of a pisco sour with the glugginess of a vanilla thickshake and the booze punch of a shot of brandy, made me shudder. I broached a compromise by using its heroes to boost a custard. While we listened to *The Little Drummer Boy*, the spices bobbed about in the bain marie, gently releasing their cosy Christmas flavours into eggs, milk and cream. The resulting custard would have been good served cold on pudding, lovely over smashed Amaretti or gingernut biscuits, or charming as a crème brûlée, if we had a blowtorch handy. That night we dribbled it over store-bought mince pies, eaten straight from the pinched foil case, which left plenty of time to sit lazily under the tree and dream of other places to go in search of St Nicholas' face.

CHRISTMAS CARPACCIO

70 g/2½ oz.
  exceptionally fresh
  firm-fleshed white fish
  per person, skinned
  and pin-boned
1 bunch dill
seeds of ½ pomegranate
salt
rye bread and butter,
  to serve

Horseradish cream
1 tablespoon freshly
  ground horseradish
  (or if you can't get any,
  horseradish in a jar)
3 tablespoons crème
  fraîche
good olive oil, for
  drizzling

Serves 6

Use a very sharp knife to carve thin slivers of the fish. It will help if the fish is very cold. Arrange about 6 or 7 thin sashimi-style slices around each plate. Cover each plate with a square of baking parchment and layer the plates on top of each other. Put the stacked fish and paper-layered plates in the fridge, with the top one weighted on top of the paper with a collection of cans. You want something heavy.

Make a horseradish cream by combining the horseradish and crème fraîche. Thin it slightly with olive oil and a splash of water; you want it to be the thickness of double/heavy cream.

To serve, remove the paper and decorate each plate of fish with sprigs of dill, pomegranate seeds and dribbles of the horseradish cream. Add a drizzle of olive oil and a sprinkle of good sea salt. Enjoy with rye bread and butter.

STUFFED PORK WITH PEAR SAUCE

1 x 2.5-kg/5½-lb. boned
  pork loin (larger if you
  have more to feed),
  with the skin scored
2 fennel bulbs, sliced
  lengthways
4 garlic cloves
125 ml/½ cup pear cider
salt and black pepper

Pear sauce
2 tablespoons butter
3 ripe pears, peeled,
  cored and diced
2 green apples, peeled
  and diced
1 teaspoon fennel seeds
1 teaspoon brown sugar
150 ml/⅔ cup pear cider

Stuffing
½ onion, finely diced
½ red apple, peeled and
  finely chopped
zest of ½ orange
1 tablespoon flat leaf
  parsley, finely chopped
1 tablespoon sage
  leaves, finely chopped
70 g/¾ cup fresh white
  breadcrumbs
1 egg, lightly beaten
35 g/¼ cup dried
  cranberries, stewed
  in 2 tablespoons hot
  cider for 10 minutes

hairdryer (optional)
kitchen string

Serves 6–8

Preheat the oven to 220°C (425°F) Gas 7. Weigh the unstuffed joint to calculate how long you should cook it for. You want 30 minutes for every 500 g/1 lb. 2 oz., plus 25 minutes extra for the crackling.

Unroll the pork and place the meat in a colander, skin-side up. Pour boiling water over the skin to encourage the crackling to fan apart, then dry the meat well (you can use a hairdryer for 5 minutes if you're particularly devoted).

Mix together the stuffing ingredients in a bowl.

Open up the pork and cut a slit 6 cm/2½ inches deep down the centre of the loin, leaving a 4-cm/ 1½-inch border at either end. Place the stuffing down the centre of the meat and roll it up with the skin on top. Tie the rolled roast with kitchen string.

Place the fennel and garlic over the bottom of a roasting tray as a trivet. Rub salt generously into the crackling and place it on top of the fennel.

Roast in the preheated oven for the first 25 minutes to encourage the crackling. Reduce the temperature to 170°C (325°F) Gas 3, pour in the cider and roast for the calculated amount of time.

To test if the meat is done, insert a skewer; the juices should run clear. Let the meat relax for 20 minutes before carving.

While the meat is resting, return the fennel to the oven to reduce further. To make the pear sauce, melt the butter in a saucepan and sauté the pears, apple and fennel seeds with the brown sugar for 5 minutes. Add the cider and stew until the fruit has broken down in the cider.

Carve the meat and serve with the stewed fennel and pear sauce.

To ensure the best crackling, make sure that you only have 5 mm/¼-inch of fat under the skin of the pork. If you have more than that, open up the fat and skin like a book and trim some of it off.

MINCE PIES

75 g/½ cup raisins
75 g/½ cup currants
75 g/½ cup sultanas
40 g/¼ cup dried cherries
  or cranberries
40 g/¼ cup dried mixed
  peel
3 tablespoons brandy or
  dark cooking sherry
2 tablespoons marmalade
50 g/3½ tablespoons
  butter, melted, or suet
3 teaspoons mixed spice
grated zest and juice of
  ½ orange

1 small cooking apple
  peeled and grated
  or diced
25 g/⅓ cup flaked/
  slivered almonds,
  finely chopped
pinch of salt
500 g/1 lb. 2 oz.
  shortcrust pastry
1 egg, lightly beaten

muffin pan, greased

Makes around 18

The night before serving, mix the dried fruit, brandy and marmalade in a bowl and cover with clingfilm/plastic wrap to allow the fruit to absorb the liquid.

The next day, combine the boozy dried fruit with the melted butter, mixed spice, orange zest and juice, apple, almonds and salt.

Roll out the pastry to 3 mm/⅛ inch thick. Cut out 8-cm/3¼-inch diameter circles to line the bases. Scrunch up the remaining pastry and re-roll to cut 7-cm/2¾-inch lids. You should be able to make around 16–18 lids and 16–18 bases.

Line the muffin pan with the pastry bases. Place 1½ tablespoons filling in each pastry base. Either place the lids over the top like a jaunty cap, or stretch to fit and crimp the sides with a fork. They don't need to completely meld with the base. Brush the tops and edges with beaten egg and use a fork to puncture the top of each pie.

Put the pies in the fridge to rest for 30 minutes. Preheat the oven to 200°C (400°F) Gas 6. Bake for 20–25 minutes until lightly golden. Leave in the pan for 10 minutes to cool, then transfer to a wire rack.

Serve the pies at room temperature with the warm custard. If you prefer to serve them warm, put them back in the muffin pan and into the oven at 150°C (300°F) Gas 2 for 15 minutes before serving.

EGGNOG CUSTARD

250 ml/1 cup milk
250 ml/1 cup double/
  heavy cream
1 cinnamon stick
1 whole nutmeg

100 g/½ cup caster/
  superfine sugar
4 egg yolks
2 tablespoons brandy
2 teaspoons cornflour/
  cornstarch

Put the milk, cream, cinnamon stick and nutmeg in a saucepan and bring to the boil. In a large heatproof bowl, whisk together the egg yolks, cornflour/cornstarch and sugar until they are duckling-yellow and fluffy.

Pour the boiling milk and cream over the eggs and sugar. Add the brandy. Whisk together until smooth. Fill the saucepan with boiling water and return it to the stove.

Put the bowl of custard on top of the boiling water. Gently stir and stir and stir, trying not to let the spices splosh out of the bowl.

Keep the heat at a gentle level and cook it slowly, stirring and giving it attention. It's ready when it feels thick enough to you. Technically, this is when it coats the back of a spoon and you can swipe through the middle and the lines will stay. Note that it will thicken further in the fridge.

Keep the cinnamon and nutmeg in the custard until you serve it – they'll keep leaching out their good flavours over time.

Cover with clingfilm/plastic wrap to prevent the custard from forming a skin.

INDEX

ACKNOWLEDGMENTS

With many thanks to:
The luminous team at RPS who worked on the book; in
particular Céline Hughes for her patience, empathy and
eagle eyes, Julia Charles and Cindy Richards for their
encouragement and enthusiasm, and Megan Smith and
Leslie Harrington for such terrific art direction. Additional
thanks to Isobel Wield for the divine photography, Andrea
Turvey for her joyful illustrations and Lizzie Harris and
Tony Hutchinson for making the food look so beautiful.
My gratitiude also goes to Tom Parker Bowles for his kind
words, my agent Clare Hulton for her guidance and Sarah
Hammond for being the grace note to it all.

Some more appreciation:
To my lovely friends scattered between two hemispheres.
A special thank you to those who helped test and taste
their way through this book; Nick and Libby, Tristan and
Nathan, Jo and Tom, Alex and Tony, May, Nicole and Joel,
Lisa and Dan, Cameron and Oliver, Liz and Sarah. Thank you.

To the kind folk who read my ramblings on eatori.com
and other places, and also to you for purchasing this book.
Thank you!

Now for some soppy ones: to Mum, Dad and Kate, for
their patience in the fledgling years when all I would eat
was white and unending support in the stretches when
things became harder to swallow. And to John, Lynne and
Linda who helped awaken me to the shining delights of
a table full of food and new versions of family.

But above all, to The Hungry One, Andrew – my
companion in all adventures. Without you, everything
is naught.